Since it is ownership that is determining the destiny of America, the answer is significant. And the answer is that a relative few own America. Only five percent of the population owns more than sixty percent of the nation's private property.

But the American land reform movement is creating stirrings of change. *The People's Land* is both an outgrowth and a tool of that movement. It presents a concise yet comprehensive picture of the problems and possibilities that confront that movement today.

The People's Land includes excerpts from many articles, studies and statements dealing with land and people in America. A selection of more than 100 historical and contemporary photographs depict the roots and the consequences of the problems and suggest the potentials of reform.

In its pages it views land reform from historical and regional perspectives, and from technological and sociological perspectives. It presents a series of concrete proposals for alternative policies and institutions—including various tax reforms, acreage limitations, land trusts, unions and co-ops—that can lead to a better society. A better society. That is the goal of the American land reform movement. That is the purpose of *The People's Land*.

The Contributors

They include Ralph Nader; Jim Hightower, director of the Agribusiness Accountability Project and author of its report *Hard Tomatoes, Hard Times*; Harry Caudill, Kentucky lawyer and author of *Night Comes to the Cumberlands*; Walter Goldschmidt, author of the 1930's landmark study of Arvin and Dinuba, California, *As You Sow*; Washington *Post* reporter Nick Kotz; Robert Rodale; Dolores Huerta, vice president of the United Farm Workers Union, AFL-CIO; Oren Lee Staley, president of the National Farmers Organization; Kirke Kickingbird, a Kiowa, and Karen Ducheneaux, a Cheyenne River Sioux, authors of *One Hundred Million Acres*; economist Paul S. Taylor; historian Paul Wallace Gates; and many others.

About the Editor

Peter Barnes is West Coast editor of *The New Republic* and a staff member of the Center for Rural Studies. He has written many articles on land-related issues and was a founder in 1971 of the National Coalition for Land Reform. He is the author of a previous book, *Pawns: The Plight of the Citizen-Soldier*, and was formerly a *Newsweek* correspondent in Washington and San Francisco.

THE PEOPLE'S LAND

THE PEOPLE'S LAND

A Reader on Land Reform in the United States

Edited by
Peter Barnes
for the
National Coalition for Land Reform

Rodale Press Book Division
Emmaus, Pa. 18049

First Printing--February, 1975   333.0973
                                    B261
B--536

Printed in the United States of America

Photo Selection and Layout by William H. Hylton

Library of Congress Cataloging in Publication Data

Barnes, Peter, 1931-   comp.
    The people's land.

    Includes index.
    1. Land reform—United States—History—Addresses, essays, lectures. 2. Land tenure—United States—History—Addresses, essays, lectures. I. National Coalition for Land Reform. II. Title.
HD191.B37   333'.00973   75-1028

ISBN 0-87857-091-8
ISBN 0-87857-093-4 pbk.

Contents

Acknowledgements viii
Introduction... ix

PART I: **Historical Perspectives**

Small Land Holders Are the Most Precious Part of a State
   Thomas Jefferson 3
Equal Rights to Land
   George Henry Evans 5
The Homestead Law in an Incongruous Land System
   Paul Wallace Gates 7
Petition for Return of Railroad Lands
   Sheldon Greene, et. al. 12
Lessons of the New Deal
   Sidney Baldwin 17
   Donald Grubbs 19

PART II: **Regional Perspectives**

Appalachia
   Harry Caudill......................................33
   Jim Branscome 37
The South
   Robert S. Browne...................................40
The Northern Plains
   Dorothy Bradley....................................44
   William L. Bryan, Jr. 46
The Midwest
   Center for Rural Affairs...........................48
   Kemp Houck...50
New England
   Geoffrey Faux......................................52
Indian Lands
   Kirke Kickingbird and Karen Ducheneaux 56

PART III: **Food, Farms and Technology**

The Industrialization of Food
   Jim Hightower......................................81

The Family Farm Is the Most Efficient Unit of Production
Angus McDonald 86
The Land Grant College Complex
Jim Hightower and Susan DeMarco 89
Organic Technology
Robert Rodale 96

PART IV: **Water and Energy**
The Battle for Acreage Limitation
Paul S. Taylor 113
Mississippi Levees and the Big Plantations
Paul Wallace Gates 118
Pumping the Ogallala Reservoir
Victor K. Ray 120
Hidden Dimensions of the Energy Crisis
Michael Perelman and Hugh Gardner 122
Energy and the Public Lands
Peter Barnes 125

PART V: **Taxes**
Sowing the Till
Jeanne Dangerfield 139
Property Tax Evasion
Ralph Nader 144
Special Farmland Assessments
Peter Barnes 148
The Severance Tax
Paul J. Kaufman 152
Taxes for Land Acquisition
John McClaughry 154

PART VI: **Small Towns and Rural Poverty**
A Tale of Two Towns
Walter Goldschmidt 171
They're Destroying Our Small Towns
Victor K. Ray 176
The People Left Behind
The President's Commission on Rural Poverty 182
The Future of Rural Policy
Geoffrey Faux 187

PART VII: **Co-Ops, Land Trusts and Land Reform**
Poor People's Co-Ops
Nick Kotz 203
The Prosperous Co-Ops
Richard Margolis 207

A Land Transfer System
 North Dakota Farmers' Union 213
The Community Land Trust
 Robert Swann 215
The Importance of Unions
 Dolores Huerta 218
The Family Farm Anti-Trust Act
 Oren Lee Staley 222
What a National Land Reform Act Might Look Like
 Center for Rural Studies 225
Buying Back the Land
 Peter Barnes 228
A Farmworker Speaks
 Manuel Leon 235
A Note About the National Coalition for Land Reform 256
Index 257

Acknowledgements

This reader would not have been possible without the enthusiastic help of many people. Most important, of course, are the authors. They graciously permitted their writings to be reprinted here, often in much-condensed form. Special appreciation also goes to Boren Chertkov, former counsel of the Senate Migratory Labor Subcommittee, who organized the Senate hearings from which many of the selections are taken.

A good number of the papers included in the reader were originally prepared for the First National Conference on Land Reform, held in San Francisco in April 1973. Thanks are therefore due to the many people who made that conference a success—especially to David Weiman.

As editor, I am also very grateful to Paul Taylor, Fred Harris, Jim Hightower, Sue Hestor, Jerry Goldstein, Berge Bulbulian, Geoffrey Faux, Elizabeth Newman and Sheldon Greene, all of whose inspiration, ideas and energy are in large part responsible for this book.

Introduction

With three out of four Americans now jammed into cities, no one pays much attention to landholding patterns in the countryside. How things have changed. A hundred years ago, land for the landless was a battle-cry. People sailed the oceans, traversed the continent and fought the Indians, all for a piece of territory they might call their own. America envisioned itself—not entirely accurately—as a nation of independent farmers, hardy, self-reliant,democratic. Others saw us this way too. De Tocqueville noted the "great equality" that existed among the immigrants who settled New England, the absence of rich, landed proprietors except in the South, and the emergence in the western settlements of "democracy arrived at its utmost limits."

Along with industrialization, however, came urbanization and the decline of the Arcadian dream. Immigrants forgot about land and thought about jobs instead; the sons and grandsons of the original pioneers began to leave the farms and join the immigrants in the cities. Radical agitation shifted from farm to factory. Frontiersmen's demands for free land and easy credit were supplanted by workers' demands for a fair wage, decent conditions and union recognition. In due course a kind of permanent prosperity was achieved, and America directed its energies outwards, not inwards. Consumers bought their food in neatly wrapped packages, at prices most of them could afford, and forgot about the land.

Why, then, should we turn back to look at our land today? One reason is that the land is still the cradle of great poverty and injustice. Another is that the beauty of the land is fast disappearing. A third is the deterioration of our cities; population dispersal in some form is a necessity. There is also a growing recognition that nagging social problems—burgeoning welfare rolls, racial tensions, the alienation of workers from their work—have not responded to treatment. Many of these problems have their roots in the land, or more precisely, in the lack of access to productive land ownership by the poor, the young and the non-white.

In the last year or two a new phrase has entered the American vocabulary, a phrase usually associated with impoverished and distant nations: *land reform*. The object of land reform is not merely to alter and control land *use*, but to alter and control land *ownership*, for it is the latter that inevitably determines the former. It is ownership—and the economics surrounding ownership—that determines whether land is farmed or paved, strip-mined or preserved, polluted or reclaimed. It is ownership that determines where people live and where they work. And, to a great degree, it is ownership that determines who is wealthy in America and who is poor, who exploits others and who gets exploited *by* others.

One third of the nation's land (including Alaska) is still publicly owned, mostly by the federal government. The rest of America, including almost all of the good farm and residential land, is in private hands. Who owns this land? What are the social, economic and environmental consequences of present land ownership patterns?

Few questions are more important for the future of America's land and people, yet there are no government reports, and almost no academic studies, that provide adequate answers. What little is known has been gleaned in recent years by students, reporters and Nader-style investigators from a maze of assessors' rolls, annual reports and obscure legal documents.

The picture that emerges is a gloomy one of highly concentrated, almost feudalistic ownership patterns. Despite the large number of Americans who own homes (or rather, who own title to mortgaged homes), the fact is that a mere five percent of the population probably owns close to two-thirds of the private property in America. In any given county, whether urban or rural, the ten largest property owners alone often own ten to fifteen percent of the assessed valuation. (Check *your* county by paying a visit to the assessor's office.) In many parts of the country, it is giant absentee landlords—timber companies, railroads, energy companies, corporate farms—that dominate the lives and livelihoods of local citizens.

How did this come about? Strange as it may seem to Americans weaned on the sanctity of private property, the notion that individuals or corporations might appropriate more land than they can use, and then charge others for the privilege of using it, is not one that has always been accepted. In fact, traditional notions of land ownership are quite different. The African's right to land, according to Julius Nyerere, prime minister of Tanzania, "was traditionally simply the right to use it. He had no other right to it, nor did it occur to him to try to claim one." The American Indian tradition was similar. "The earth was created without lines of demarcation," said Chief Joseph of the Nez Perce, "and it is no man's business to divide it." Indian and Hispano villages in Mexico developed around what was called the *ejido*—lands held by the village in perpetuity for common use by its members.

The American idea of private property in land derives from imperial Rome. When the Roman republic first emerged from the veils of history, each citizen possessed a small homestead, which was inalienable, and enjoyed rights to the general domain. It was from the public domain that the patrician families began to carve their great estates. Later they absorbed the homesteads as well, forcing the small proprietors to become either rent-paying *coloni* or slaves, or to flee to the cities and newly conquered provinces. From Italy the *latifundia* spread to Sicily, Spain and Gaul, as military leaders were rewarded with large grants of land. Eventually, in the view of many historians, the social polarization brought about by the *latifundia* undermined Rome's strength and led to its demise.

From the moment of independence the United States faced the question of how to dispose of its seemingly limitless lands. There was never any doubt that private, as opposed to common ownership, would prevail. The debate was between those, like Thomas Jefferson, who favored equitable distribution of small parcels to settlers, and most of the other politicians of the day, who willingly and eagerly bestowed land upon wealthy interests and speculators—including themselves.

The history of the giveaway of America's public lands—hundreds of millions of acres over a century and a half—constitutes one of the most inglorious scandals in the annals of modern man. Fraud, chicanery and corruption were there aplenty, but even more grievous was the disregard for the social consequences of uneven land distribution. Congress did at times enact such foresighted measures as the Homestead Act of 1862 and the Reclamation Act of 1902, granting title to actual settlers who would cultivate up to 160 acres. More commonly, however, Congress and the State legislatures authorized the wholesale disposal of public lands to railroads, cattle barons and assorted speculators.

The social consequences of such wanton giveaways were not limited to the quick enrichment of a fortunate few. The pattern of large landholdings, accompanied by racial exploitation, became ensconced in the West and the South. The Jeffersonian vision of a democracy of small freeholders was scarcely tested. Great disparities of wealth and power were etched into the national landscape. Eventually the landless and powerless of rural America began drifting into the cities, ill-prepared, poorly educated and deprived of cultural roots. The path was paved for the urban crisis and the corporate feudalism that we have today in rural areas.

It may well be too late to build a society based on democratic egalitarian and ecological principles, but that is the goal of the American land reform movement. It is an awesome challenge, since the forces of privilege and despoliation are immensely powerful. But stirrings of change are abroad in the land. The relationships between people and land are coming under renewed scrutiny. There is great interest in returning to rural areas, in organic farming, in local ownership of land and resources. Land reform groups in all parts of the country, each in their own way, are engaged in a kind of two-pronged effort. On the one hand, they are vigorously chipping away at the policies and institutions that separate us from and devour the land. On the other hand, they are building alternative institutions and advocating alternative policies that can lead us toward a better society.

This reader is both an outgrowth and a tool of the land reform movement. It includes excerpts from many articles, studies and statements dealing with land and people in America. The selections are of varying length and cover a wide range of topics. All are clearly written and eminently readable. Taken together, they present a concise yet comprehensive picture of the problems and possibilities that confront the land reform movement in the United States today.

Part I
Historical Perspectives

Small Land Holders
Are the Most Precious
Part of a State

Thomas Jefferson was an enlightened Virginia slave owner who was one of the earliest and most articulate spokesmen for distributing land widely to small holders. Unfortunately, the auctioning off of public lands to speculators rather than settlers quickly became a favorite method of raising government revenue, and the Jeffersonian vision of freeholder democracy was honored more in public rhetoric than in public policy.

Here, in a letter to James Madison dated October 28, 1785, Jefferson makes the case for distributing land to those who wish to till it.

Thomas Jefferson

Legislators cannot invent too many devices for subdividing property, only taking care to let their subdivisions go hand in hand with the natural affections of the human mind. The descent of property of every kind therefore to all the children, or to all the brothers and sisters, or other relations in equal degree, is a politic measure, and a practicable one. Another means of silently lessening the inequality of property is to exempt all from taxation below a certain point, and to tax the higher portions of property in geometrical progression as they rise.

Whenever there is in any country, uncultivated lands and unemployed poor, it is clear that the laws of property have been so far extended as to violate natural right. The earth is given as a commonstock for man to labour and live on. If for the encouragement of industry we allow it to be appropriated, we must take care that other employment be provided to those excluded from the appropriation. If we do not the fundamental right to labour the earth returns to the unemployed.

It is too soon yet in our country to say that every man who

3

cannot find employment but who can find uncultivated land shall be at liberty to cultivate it, paying a moderate rent. But it is not too soon to provide by every possible means that as few as possible shall be without a little portion of land. The small land holders are the most precious part of a state.

Equal Rights to Land

The early part of the 19th century saw a great westward surge of population. Thousands of squatters staked claims to unsettled lands, only to be driven off by the Army or avaricious speculators. The Pre-emption Acts of 1830 and 1841 enabled squatters to buy title to up to 160 acres at $1.25 an acre, but this did not put an end to wholesale speculation and fraud in the disposal of public lands, nor did it benefit those who lacked the money to travel to and pay for the land. By the 1840's, a widespread movement had emerged for free homesteads to settlers. George Henry Evans, a New York labor editor, was one of the leading free soil advocates. He urged an end to all selling of public lands and the free distribution of no more than 160 acres per family to actual settlers and farmers. He also wanted the government to pay for transportation to the land and equipment to farm it.

The following excerpt is from The Working Man's Advocate, *March 16, 1844.*

George Henry Evans—————————————————————

The leading measure that we shall propose in this paper is the Equal Right of every man to the free use of a sufficient portion of the Earth to till for his subsistence. If man has a right to live, as all subsistence comes from the earth, he has a right, in a state of nature, to a portion of its spontaneous products; in a state of civilization, to a portion of the earth to till for his subsistence. This right is now, no matter why, in possession of a comparative few, many of whom possess not only a sufficiency, but a superfluity, of land: yet we propose not to divest them of that superfluity, against their consent. We simply propose that the inequality extend no further; that Government shall no longer traffic or permit traffic in that which is the property of no man or government; that the Land shall be left, as Nature dictates, free to the use of those who choose to bestow their labor upon it.

We propose that the Public Lands of the States and of the

United States shall be free to actual settlers, and to actual settlers only; that townships of six miles square shall be laid out in Farms and Lots, of any vacant one of which a man, not possessed of other land, may take possession and keep same during his life or pleasure, and with the right to sell his improvements, at any time, to any one not possessed of other land....

We shall be told, perhaps, as we have been told occasionally by persons who had not reflected on the subject, that the public lands are so cheap now as to be accessible to all industrious persons who desire to settle on them. It is not so. Though the nominal price of the lands is one dollar and twenty-five cents an acre, the real price to the actual settler is nearer ten dollars an acre, unless he chooses to become a squatter and trust to Congress for the privilege of purchasing his land at the government price; for the speculator, under the present system, goes ahead of the settler, picks out the best and most eligibly suited tracts, pays for them with paper money (itself a monstrous cheat) or its profits, and when the actual settler comes, he must either pay the speculator's price or go further into the wilderness, where he must struggle for years under the disadvantage of conveying his surplus products over bad roads to a distant market.

But suppose that the settler could obtain lands near a market at the government price, they would still be as inaccessible to the bulk of our surplus laboring population as if they were in the hands of the speculators. Some few become settlers under the present system; a few more might become so if speculation in land were entirely prohibited; but it needs that the lands should be free, in order that the surplus laborers may be absorbed; for the expense of removal to the lands, and of the necessary stock and provisions to bring them into successful cultivation, is more than many could meet.

The Homestead Law in an Incongruous Land System

In 1862, after many years of popular agitation, Congress finally authorized the free distribution of 160-acre tracts to settlers who would live on them and improve them. This was the famous Homestead Act, but it came too late and was very disappointing in its results.

In the following article, excerpted from the American Historical Review *[1936],* Paul Wallace Gates *examines the actual consequences of the Homestead Act. Gates, who now teaches history at Cornell University, is one of the leading authorities on U.S. public land policy. In 1972, 36 years after publication of this article, Gates was invited to testify before the Senate Migratory Labor Subcommittee. There, he expounded a gloomy long-range view of American history. "This country once had opportunities for land ownership that attracted population from lands of great estates owned by an aristocracy and worked by landless peasants," Gates told the Senators. "Are we now coming full circle? Are the lines Oliver Goldsmith wrote of 18th Century England now becoming applicable to America?*

'Ill fares the land, to hastening ills a prey,
When wealth accumulates, and men decay.' "

Paul Wallace Gates

The principle of free homesteads for settlers had long been the goal for which the West had struggled, and as each succeeding land law, more liberal than its predecessor, was passed, that goal came constantly nearer until, in 1862, it was attained. So generous seemed this policy in contrast with the earlier one of regarding the lands as a source of revenue, and so significant did it appear prospectively, that it became the subject of eulogy at the outset.

Consequently there was built up around the law a halo of political and economic significance which has greatly magnified the importance to be attributed to it and which has misled practically every historian and economist who has dealt with land policies. It is the purpose of this paper to show that the Homestead Law did not completely change our land system, that its adoption merely superimposed upon the old land system a principle out of harmony with it, and that until 1890 the old and the new constantly clashed.

From the outset the cards were stacked against the efficient and successful operation of the Homestead Law. Other acts in existence in 1862 greatly limited its application, and new laws further restricting it were subsequently enacted. The administration of the law, both in Washington and in the field, was frequently in the hands of people unsympathetic to its principle, and Western interests, though lauding the act, were ever ready to subvert it. The existence of the Preemption Act and its later variations, the Desert Land Act, the Timber Culture Act, the Timber and Stone Act, the land grants to railroads and states, the cash sale system, the Indian land policy, the acts granting land warrants to ex-soldiers or their heirs, and the Agricultural College Act of 1862, which granted millions of acres of land scrip to Eastern states, tended to make it practically as easy for speculators to engross huge areas of land after 1862 as before.

The retention of the Preemption Act and the commutation clause of the Homestead Law made it possible for timber dealers, cattle grazers, mining interests, and speculators to continue to acquire lands through the use of dummy entrymen, false swearing, and often, the connivance of local land officers. That this was done on a large scale is evident by the frequent and sometimes pathetic admissions of the apparently helpless Land Commissioners. The Desert Land Act, the Timber Culture Act and the Timber and Stone Act provided even greater opportunities for dummy entrymen to enter lands and assign them to hidden land engrossers. The palpable frauds committed and the large areas transferred under these acts and their interference with the homestead principle lead one to suspect that their enactment and retention were the results of political pressure by interested groups.

The continuation of the policy of granting to the states federal lands within their borders was likewise contrary to the homestead principle. With the exception of the swamp-land grants, the purpose of these donations was to provide the states with a valuable commodity, the sale of which would produce revenue or endowment for educational and other state institutions. Over 72 million acres were granted to states which came into the Union after 1862, while other states had their grants increased subsequent to the enactment of the Homestead Law. It is safe to say that over 140 million acres of land were in the hands of the states for disposition after 1862. The philosophy behind the grants, and frequently the conditions embedded in the donations, required their sale at the highest market price. The states were prevented, therefore, from giving homesteads to settlers, and the prices asked for their lands, with the exception of the swamp lands, which were generally sold at low prices or granted to railroads, made them the prey of speculators. It is true that limitations were sometimes placed on the amount of land which individuals could purchase, but dummy entrymen were usually employed to circumvent such restrictions.

The maintenance of the cash sale system after the Homestead Law went into operation did even greater violence to the principle of free lands. It is not generally appreciated that there were available in 1862 for cash sale 83,919,649 acres of land. This figure was later increased to well over 100 million acres by the opening up of new lands to the auction and cash sale system. Throughout the sixties and seventies and, indeed, until 1888, the government continued to offer land at auction in Oregon, Washington, California, Kansas, Nebraska, Colorado, New Mexico and in practically all of the states in the Lakes region and in the Mississippi Valley where it still had land. It is true that after 1870 most of the land so offered was timbered, but by then a goodly portion of the arable lands had been surveyed and opened to sale. The richest and most fertile sections of Kansas, Nebraska, Missouri, California, Washington and Oregon were thus open to the cash purchaser after the enactment of the Homestead Law, and great landed estates were acquired through outright purchase in these states.

Little attention has been devoted by historians to the Indian lands and yet there is a story involved in their disposition totally at variance with the conventional account of the era of free land. At the time the Homestead Law was passed, the government was following the policy of concentrating the Indians on reservations where they would be in less conflict with white settlers. The rights of the Indians in lands claimed by them were recognized and, when they were persuaded to leave a hunting area over which they claimed ownership to dwell in a reservation, they were generally compensated for their lands either by the federal government or by a purchaser acting with the consent of the government. Some of the lands were ceded outright to the government for a consideration; others were ceded in trust, the lands to be sold for the benefit of the Indians; the disposition of still others to railroads was authorized in a number of treaties.

The only consistent rule concerning them was that they must be sold for a consideration, which, of course, denied to the homesteader the right to enter them free.

The amount of land in Indian reservations or claimed by the Indians in 1862 was probably 175 million acres. The land was scattered throughout the Western states, but large amounts were concentrated in the states of Kansas and Nebraska and the Dakota and Indian territories into which settlers were eagerly pressing in the sixties, seventies and eighties, or where they looked longingly for lands. At the outset, these lands were sold in large blocks to groups of capitalists and railroads, without being offered in small lots. Slightly later they were appraised, generally at high valuations, offered at auction and sold to the highest bidders. Still later, some of the Indian lands were sold in small tracts to settlers, a slight concession to the homeseekers.

With over 125 million acres of railroad lands, 140 million acres of state lands, 100 million acres of Indian lands and 100 million acres of federal lands for sale in large or small blocks, and with the opportunities for evasion of the Homestead and Preemption laws and their variations outlined above, it is obvious that there were few obstacles in the way of speculation and land monopolization after 1862. As before, it was still possible for foresighted speculators to precede settlers into the frontier, purchase the best lands and hold them for the anticipated increase in value which the succeeding wave of settlers would give to them. It has heretofore been maintained that the existence of free land after 1862 greatly diminished the speculator's chances of profit and consequently limited their activities. This view will not bear careful scrutiny. Except for the squatters' claims, the speculators were generally able to secure the most desirable lands, that is, those easily brought under cultivation, fertile and close to timber, water, markets and lines of communication. The subsequent settler had the choice of buying at the speculators' prices, from the land-grant railroads which held their alternate tracts at equally high prices, from the states whose land policies were less generous that those of the federal government, or of going farther afield to exercise his homestead privilege where facilities for social and economic intercourse were limited.

Not only were the best agricultural lands being snapped up by speculators but the richest timberlands remaining in the possession of the United States were being rapidly entered by large dealers during the post-Civil War period. There were three areas in which vast amounts of timberland were still owned by the federal government, the Lake states, the Gulf states with Arkansas, and the Pacific Coast states. In each of these three regions, millions of acres of pine, spruce, hemlock and fir were available for cash entry, and in the Pacific area lands covered with the rich redwood and other trees peculiar to that region had been, or were just being, brought into the market. In the timberlands of these three sections some of the largest purchases by speculators or lumbermen took place.

Further details concerning the widespread speculative activity in public lands—both agricultural and timbered—after the passage of the Homestead Act are unnecessary; it is clear that speculation and land engrossment were not retarded by the act. Homeseekers in the West, being unwilling to go far afield from means of transportation or to settle upon the inferior lands remaining open to homestead, and lacking capital with which to purchase farms and to provide equipment for them, were frequently forced to become tenants on the lands of speculators. Thus farm tenancy developed in the frontier stage at least a generation before it would have appeared had the homestead system worked properly.

It was not entirely necessary, however, for speculators to resort to these illegal and fraudulent methods of acquiring land, since Congress proceeded to aid their schemes by enacting a series of laws which went far toward vitiating the principle of land for the landless. By continuing after 1862 the policy of granting lands to railroads to encourage their construction, Congress from the outset struck a severe blow at the principle of free homesteads. In the eight years after the passage of the Homestead Law, five times as much land was granted to railroads as had been given in the twelve preceeding years; 127,628,000 acres were granted between 1862 and 1871 to aid in the extension of the railroad net and 2,000,000 acres were granted for wagon roads and canals. Such imperial generosity was at the expense of future homesteaders who must purchase the land. As it was necessary to withdraw all lands from entry in the regions through which such roads were projected to prevent speculators from anticipating the railroads in making selections of land, and as the routes were rarely definitely established when the grants were made, more than double this amount of land was withdrawn from entry and remained unavailable to settlement for a long period of years.

Petition for Return of Railroad Lands

Although public lands suitable for homesteading were almost entirely staked out by the early 1900's, nearly a third of the land area in the United States is still owned by the federal government. Much of this land is leased to private individuals and corporations for mining, timber cutting and cattle grazing, in ways that are not always consistent with the public interest [See, for example, the article on Energy and the Public Lands, *page 125.]*

Another public land issue that is still very much alive involves land granted to the railroads more than a century ago. In 1972, the National Coalition for Land Reform asked the Interior Department to investigate the legal status of these railroad lands. Though its petition was supported by numerous Congressmen and Senators, the Interior Department has yet to act.

The following document, an administrative complaint to Interior Secretary Rogers C. B. Morton, presents the case for returning railroad lands to the public and opening them up for settlement at $2.50 an acre.

Sheldon Greene, David Kirkpatrick, David M. Madway and Richard Pearl

During the third quarter of the 19th Century, Congress gave the American railroads an empire of approximately 150 million acres, almost eight percent of the total land area of the United States. The purpose of this giveaway was two-fold: to finance construction of new lines, and to encourage settlement of the granted lands by small farmers.

To assure that these objectives were attained, many of the grants were subject to a critical condition: in the event that the railroad line for which the grant was made was not completed, all lands granted to finance its construction were to be forfeited to the United States. Several grants contained a further condition requiring that patented lands be sold to settlers at a price not to exceed $1.25 per acre, or in some cases, $2.50 per acre. Three of the largest grants, in the most unequivocal terms, set forth the sale requirement as follows:

> All such lands so granted by this section, which shall not be sold or disposed of by said company within three years after the entire road shall be completed, shall be subject to settlement and preemption, like other lands, at a price not exceeding one dollar and twenty-five cents per acre, to be paid to said company. ₁

What the granting acts contemplated was a scheme that would both encourage construction of the railroads and prevent those same railroads from holding in perpetuity a land area equal in size to the states of Florida and California combined.

The limited nature of the railroads' interest in the land was best stated by the United States Supreme Court in its landmark opinion in *Oregon and California R. Co. v. U.S.*, 243 U.S. 549 (1917). The Court said that once the railroad lines were completed "the interest that the granting acts conferred upon the railroad was $2.50 per acre," and the rights to sell at that price were nothing more than "aides to the duty of transmitting the land to settlers."

In the late 19th and early 20th Centuries, innumerable frauds, mistakes and violations of the terms of the land grant covenants were disclosed by periodic inquiries.

Before 1890, Congress had adopted 15 special forfeiture acts causing over 25 million acres to revert to the public domain because railroads failed to complete rights of way or in some cases even to begin them. Nevertheless, government studies disclosed that the special forfeiture acts returned at best only half the public land which could have reverted to the public due to railroad defaults.

In 1890 Congress declared a general forfeiture of all lands granted for the construction of lines which were not yet completed and in violation of their completion date. Under the act the lands were to be restored to the public domain.

Perhaps the most extensive litigation was the *Oregon and California* case, cited above, which found its way to the Supreme Court not once but twice. The litigation centered on over two million acres of land granted to a subsidiary of the Southern Pacific. The Court found that some of that land had been disposed of by the railroad in parcels larger than 160 acres and at prices substantially in excess of $1.25 per acre. The railroad maintained that since it had the power to mortgage the land, it could also sell the land on foreclosure free of maximum size and price conditions. The implication of this argument was that financing arrangements could be engineered to "wash" the grant lands of restrictions imposed by law. The Supreme Court rejected that suggestion, stating that its effect would be

> to declare that covenants violated are the same as covenants performed, wrongs done the same as rights exercised and, by confounding these essential distinctions give to the transgression of the law what its observers alone are entitled to.

Most significant, perhaps, for the present day is the Court's declaration that the railroad had no right to harvest timber or extract minerals from grant lands but rather held such lands solely "for the purpose of transmission to actal settlers" at the price established in the granting statutes.

In another case concerning these timber and mineral rights, the Southern Pacific obtained patents to known oil lands although the grant had expressly prohibited it from receiving mineral lands. Evidence at the trial established that the Southern Pacific's land agent was aware of the oil-bearing potential of the land but had been advised by his superiors to file false affidavits claiming that the land was strictly agricultural. The Supreme Court found that the lands had been fraudulently obtained and cancelled the patents. [2]

Notwithstanding the General Forfeiture Act and numerous court cases, the Pacific railroads still held 12 million acres as of 1940. In that year Congress gave up the government's right to reduced rates and the railroads, in return, relinquished claims to grant lands.

The legislative history of the Transportation Act of 1940 indicates that the railroads released

> claims against the United States to lands, interests in lands, compensation or reimbursement on account of lands or interests in lands which had been granted, claimed to have been granted, or which it was claimed should have been granted to such carrier, under any grant from the United States. [3]

Similarly, the committee hearings confirm the purpose of the bill to obtain the return to the public domain of the remaining 12,286,517 acres held by the railroads. The results, however, were less than Congress intended.

According to the Interior Department, the implementation of the reversion provision returned 8 million of the 12 million acres to the public domain. Yet statistics indicate that in fact the largest railroad landowner, the Southern Pacific, never returned its land.

In 1939, prior to the Transportation Act, the Southern

Pacific had 3,895,000 acres. In 1971, after the ostensible reversion to the United States of the remaining land grants, the Southern Pacific still had 3,845,000 acres. The following facts about some of that land raise questions of sufficient magnitude to warrant an investigation by the Department of the Interior of all grant lands presently held by railroads.

(1) The Central and Western Pacific Companies, subsidiaries of the Southern Pacific, hold lands between San Francisco and Lake Tahoe in California pursuant to a federal grant. The grant explicitly required that the land be sold to settlers at no more than $1.25 an acre.

The rail line referred to in the condition was completed before 1900. Therefore, in light of the land management condition of the grant, the remaining land should have been, but was not, made available for homestead purposes.

(2) Certain Southern Pacific holdings in the San Joaquin Valley of California were conditioned upon the completion of a line from San Jose to Needles. Construction was completed between San Jose and Tres Pinos, and between Alcalde and Needles, leaving an 84-mile gap between Tres Pinos and Alcalde. Under the terms of the grant, the entire Southern Pacific holdings in the area deriving from the specific grant should be forfeited pursuant to the Act of 1890.

(3) In 1970, the Southern Pacific earned $24 million from timber and agricultural leases on some of its 3,845,000 acres, as well as from mineral rights on an additional 1.3 million acres. In the *Oregon and California* case, the Supreme Court specifically rejected the railroad's claim that it could legally exploit the land commercially.

The above examples suggest that railroads are currently holding grant lands which their original grant (1) required them to sell to the public subject to maximum size and price limitations, (2) required them to return to the federal government, or (3) forbid them to exploit commercially as they now appear to be doing.

Such illegal uses support nullification of patents and return of the land to the public domain, as well as a careful investigation of the propriety of demanding an accounting for profits which rightfully belong to the United States.

Petitioners therefore request the Department of the Interior to initiate an immediate and detailed investigation into the status of the railroad land grants and the disposition of the railroad lands to ascertain the extent of noncompliance with conditions applicable to original land grantees and their successors in interest.

Petitioners believe that such a detailed investigation will

demonstrate the propriety of some or all of the following remedial actions:

(1) An administrative or court order requiring the railroads to make available to petitioners and others similarly situated a reasonable amount of arable land at prices not to exceed $2.50 an acre;

(2) Forfeiture by said railroads to the federal government of lands held in violation of law. Such lands would then enter the public domain and be opened to settlement under the Homestead and related acts, or retained for national forests, wildlife refuges, open spaces, and other uses in the public interest;

(3) An accounting for, and reimbursement to the general treasury by said railroads of all profits made from uses of such lands prohibited by the land grant laws.

1 12 Stat. 489, § 3 (Union and Central Pacific); 16 Stat. 47, § 1 (Oregon and California subsidiary of the Central Pacific); 16 Stat. 573, § 9 (Texas Pacific).

2 *U.S. v. Southern Pacific R. Co.*, 251 U.S. 1 (1919).

3 House Committee Miscellaneous Reports II, April 26, 1940, Conference Report Accompanying S 2009, 76 Cong. 3rd Sess. HR Report H2016 at 87.

Lessons of the New Deal

The last concerted effort to apply land reform in the United States occurred during President Franklin D. Roosevelt's administration. This effort, which was led by the Farm Security Administration, was for several years extremely successful in helping poor people stay on the land, getting new farmers started, and setting up cooperatives. Eventually, the New Deal got sidetracked by World War II and the political opponents of land reform were able to put the FSA out of business.

The following two selections present varying views on the lesson of the New Deal. Sidney Baldwin, a professor of political science at California State College in Fullerton, argues that the FSA was a valiant effort whose failure does not mean that future land reform efforts will be doomed to similar defeat. Donald H. Grubbs, a history professor at the University of the Pacific, Stockton, California, contends that the New Deal was not really reformist at all. Rather, he claims, it strengthened the landed aristocracy in the South and helped drive millions of poor people off the land.

Both statements are taken from a panel discussion at the First National Conference on Land Reform in 1973. Fuller discussion of the authors' views can be found in Baldwin, Poverty and Politics: The Rise and Decline of the Farm Security Administration [*University of North Carolina Press, 1968*], *and Grubbs,* Cry from the Cotton: The Southern Tenant Farmers Union and the New Deal [*University of North Carolina Press, 1971*].

Sidney Baldwin

The evolution of the Farm Security Administration was a long and complex process. From the beginning of the Roosevelt administration, a variety of programs were developed to improve the quality of rural life in America. Most of them were hurriedly conceived and set up. In 1935, largely under the inspiration of Under-Secretary of Agriculture Rexford Guy Tugwell, President Roosevelt, without congressional authorization, set up the Resettlement Administration and placed it in Tugwell's hands.

For two years this new agency, the predecessor of the FSA,

17

administered an astonishing variety of programs. For the purchase and retirement of worn-out land and the resettlement of dislocated families, it administered a *land program*. For poor families returning to the land or making a new beginning on better land, it carried out a *rural resettlement program*. For families with modest incomes, there was a *suburban resettlement program*. And for families who needed more than land, there was a *rural rehabilitation program* that involved a cluster of financial, social and technical remedies.

By 1936 it became apparent that basic legislation was needed to strengthen the political support for these programs. There began a serious effort to secure a legislative mandate from Congress which ended, after many failures and frustrations, with passage in 1937 of the Bankhead-Jones Farm Tenant Act. The Act created the Farm Security Administration to conduct a comprehensive attack on almost every aspect of rural poverty. This attack—which lasted from 1937 to 1942—was not developed in accordance with some grand design. Rather, one thing led pragmatically to another. For instance, when the granting of credit to a low-income farm family was not enough to raise it from poverty, rural rehabilitation was added. When poor farming practices were found to be related to ill health, a medical care program was introduced. And when it was discovered that providing temporary shelter for migratory farm workers in labor camps was not enough, the FSA expanded its program to include transportation to jobs, technical training and assistance to workers in negotiations with their employers.

Within a few years, the agency became one of the largest and most influential in the federal government. It operated in over 2,000 rural counties, employed more than 19,000 specialists and served more than 800,000 farm families.

Wherever the FSA operated, and whatever it did, it seemed to touch sensitive nerves. By violating the delicate Southern protocol governing the relations between blacks and whites, it was perceived as a challenge to "the Southern way of life." By earning the distrust of the conservative farm organizations and the state colleges of agriculture, it was seen as a threat to the established power structure in rural America.

Beginning in 1942, the FSA suffered a long period of political attack and emasculation. Civil service status, for instance, was denied to FSA employees. Vigorous leaders of the agency were forced to resign. The agency was accused of "Communism" and "Un-Americanism." By 1945 the FSA was a forlorn spectacle held in contempt by its foes and despair by its friends. A Congress that was becoming ever more conservative allowed the agency to languish for another year. Then, during the summer of 1946, the

Farmers Home Administration Act was passed by Congress and signed by President Truman. The FSA was abolished and in its place was set up the more cautious and docile Farmers Home Administration within the Department of Agriculture.

The so-called "lessons of history" are not engraved permanently in writing on the wall. The true meaning of history changes from generation to generation, and so it would be a mistake to conclude from the fate of the Farm Security Administration that all future land reform efforts will be doomed to similar defeat.

The 1970s are not the 1930s or 1940s. We now know much more about the causes and cures of poverty and land degradation. There are currents in the air today that suggest that perhaps a new day may be dawning.

Donald H. Grubbs —————————————

It is commonplace for Americans to consider Franklin Roosevelt's New Deal as the most reformist era of any in our history. Actually, the roots both of today's urban ghettos and of reactionary agribusiness lie largely in the New Deal. Roosevelt not only drove sharecroppers off the land, but promoted with his subsidies today's right-wing farming industry.

To understand the path that leads from Roosevelt and Henry Wallace to Earl Butz and Richard Nixon, we have to begin with some working definitions of what conservatism is, what reform means, and how we can judge radicalism. A conservative program is not one which keeps everything exactly the same, or returns us to a simpler day. Rather, the essence of conservatism is the acceptance of changes in detail or method in order to preserve society's dominant incentives and institutions. Changes can be called progressive only to the extent that they distribute riches—material and otherwise—more equitably, and they can be called radical only to the extent that they alter fundamental values.

By these definitions, and with special attention to the American countryside, the New Deal was seldom progressive and certainly not radical; on the contrary, it strengthened traditional incentives and institutions.

Virtually everyone knows that vast subsidies to agriculture began with the New Deal, but few of us are aware that even before World War II, the richer agricultural areas received more money than the poorer ones, and the wealthier ranchers and planters profited more than family farmers. Nowhere was this tendency more marked or more disastrous than in the South. The racist plantation landlords who in the past had been willing to allow their sharecroppers to keep only half of the cotton they raised, were paid by the New Deal to withdraw a third of their acreage from production. But the subsidy on each withdrawn acre was not split half and half; the split was initially eight to one in favor of the landlord. Often, the tenant or cropper didn't even receive the pittance that the AAA was supposed to allow him. And since wage laborers were entitled to nothing at all, a monetary inducement was offered to Southern planters to demote their workers to the insecure status of casual labor, employed only seasonally. Eventually millions drifted out of the South altogether, probably the largest government-impelled population movement in all our history.

One suspects immediately that so humane a man as Roosevelt must have felt forced into such a program by his political dependence on Southern conservatives. But would they have actually deserted the New Deal coalition if, for example, safeguards against tenant eviction, fairer distribution of farm subsidies, or a greater commitment to agricultural cooperatives had been made? This seems unlikely, since their allegiance to Democratic farm policy was overwhelming and unwavering.

The New Deal's strengthening of individual and corporate, rather than cooperative or collective, agriculture had two dramatic consequences. First, it meant that the heavily capitalized, tax-subsidized enterprises of the future would view labor as a cost to be cut rather than as a productive factor. The New Deal thus led America not toward productivity and purchasing power on the land, but toward waste and welfare in our cities.

Second, the New Deal's strengthening of established institutions in agriculture was ominous politically. It was already apparent that the Farmer-Labor parties were disintegrating, that the National Farmers' Union would never win major influence, and that farmworkers were of marginal concern. Therefore, to rebuild agriculture without reconstructing it meant building power for the right-wing American Farm Bureau Federation and its allies. This second disaster, though less frequently noted than the first, may possibly rank close to it in importance.

The new nation offered land for the landless.

T. L. Gettings. *Oregon, 1974.*

Oklahoma Historical Society. *The Cherokee Outlet,
guaranteed in perpetuity to the Cherokee Indians, is opened
to settlement, September 16, 1893.*

The Indians were displaced,
the sod broken.

William Henry Jackson, Hayden Survey, National Archives. *Looking west over the
plains of the Sweetwater River from the Devil's Gate; Fremont County, Wyoming, 1871.*

U.S. Signal Corps., National Archives. *Crow Indian on reservation, 1897.*

Solomon D. Butcher Collection, Nebraska State Historical Society. *Family and their sod house; Nebraska, ca. 1889.*

But Jeffersonian democracy proved a myth,

USDA. *Settlers; Nebraska, 1887.*

USDA. *Farmers with their corn crop; Nebraska, 1904.*

National Archives. *First sale of lots; Imperial Valley, California, April 12, 1904.*

Arthur Rothstein, FSA. *Oklahoma dust storm, 193*

USDA. *After dust storm; South Dakota, 1935.*

... as the Great Depression and the dust bowl recreated

John Vachon, FSA. *Ozark Mountain farm family; Missouri, 1940.*

Dorothea Lange, FSA. *Abandoned
farmhouse on large mechanized
cotton farm; Texas, 1938.*

Dorothea Lange, FSA. *Towards Los Angeles; California, 1937.*

Dorothea Lange, FSA. *Migrant families from Missouri look for work in California pea fields; 1936.*

...the dispossessed masses.

Dorothea Lange, FSA. *Daughter of migrant Tennessee coal miner; California, 1936.*

Dorothea Lange , FSA. *California, 1937.*

Part II
Regional Perspectives

Appalachia

Who owns the land and resources of the United States? Though the cast of characters differs from region to region, the plot is depressingly the same: big absentee owners exploit both land and people with little regard for the environment or human well-being.

In Appalachia, the biggest land owners are the energy companies. These giant corporations have depleted the land of its wealth and left the people poor. In the following article, Harry Caudill explains how this happened and proposes a remedy: the public utility district. Caudill is an attorney in Whitesburg, Kentucky, and the author of My Land is Dying *and other books about Appalachia. The article is taken from his statement to the First National Conference on Land Reform.*

A new kind of absentee owner—not just in Appalachia but in many rural areas—is the second home or resort developer. Jim Branscome writes about the impact of these "invaders" on the poor mountain folk of Appalachia. Branscome works with the Highlander Research Center in New Market, Tennessee. The article published here first appeared in the Mountain Eagle.

Harry Caudill

Appalachia's history has bequeathed to us two very severe difficulties respecting land ownership. They combine to doom the vast region to continuing exploitation and poverty.

After the Civil War industrialists were able to glimpse the outlines of the nation's coming growth and they foresaw the indispensability of Appalachian coal. Agents of coal and iron companies and ambitious speculators moved in to corner title to the mineral deposits the geologists had located. These mineral buyers soon learned two things about Appalachia: the mineral wealth was vast, varied and of high quality; and the mountaineers were so poor and undiscerning that they would sell cheaply.

Some genius produced a printed deed form with appropriate blank spaces for names, dates and boundary descriptions, and

33

purchasing got underway. Prices ranged from as little as a dime to as much as five or six dollars per acre, and the "northern" or "broad-form" deed was recorded thousands of times in hundreds of deed books. These documents transferred to absentee steel and coal corporations and to huge holding companies ownership of "all coal, oil and gas, all salt and salt water, all stone, slate and shale, all mineral and metallic substances, and all combinations of the same lying upon or within" the lands. The deeds conveyed, also, sweeping privileges to operate mines and wells, to store wastes and residues, to pollute and divert surface and underground waters, and to do any and all things deemed "necessary or convenient" in order to get out the minerals and send them to market.

The sellers, for themselves and their successors, waived all claims and demands for damages resulting from mining, drilling, the laying of pipelines and so on. They preserved for themselves and all other mountaineers who might claim the land in coming centuries only "the surface of the land, together with the right to use same for such agricultural purposes as are not inconsistent with" the rights of the mineral owners. Thus the majority of land-owning mountaineers became by contract and law little more than tenants by sufferance in their own hills.

The arrogance of Appalachia's new corporate landlords knew—and knows—no bounds. State mining laws were weak and weakly enforced. Immense slate dumps piled up near hundreds of tipples and sent palls of black, sulfurous smoke down into towns and across farms. The tipples rained clouds of dust and grit onto the same communities. The trees were cut down for lumber and mine props and flood waters roared down the denuded slopes to drown and sicken. The companies sliced off mountain tops to get the upper coal seams and "contour-stripped" and augered at lower levels, choking rivers with mud, filling lakes with silt, and emptying entire valleys. Underground mines became the deadliest on earth, killing men at four or five times the rate experienced in the pits of Holland, Germany and England.

Coal trains, lumber trains, barges, trucks and pipelines have carried half a trillion dollars worth of raw materials out of Appalachia in the last 140 years. Scores of counties have been systematically plundered for wood, limestone, talc, marble, clays, copper, iron ore, coal and gas. As the much touted "energy crisis" deepens the exploitation will steadily worsen unless the region's minerals—particularly its coal—are put to work in new and rejuvenative ways.

The people of Appalachia can bring their counties to economic health and social well-being by an enlargement of a device pioneered in the state of Washington—the public utility district. This tool has been thoroughly tested in that state and would involve little pioneering in Appalachia.

Forty years ago much of the state of Washington was cut-over timber land and semi-desert. After the lumber companies had logged the forests, fire swept through the wood residues leaving the earth blackened and naked. Erosion did immeasurable harm, but slowly the land healed itself with thickets as nature struggled to restore her forests. Thousands of people moved away and some of the counties were threatened with extinction. The people who remained came to the desperate realization that they, too, must abandon the territory or rebuild their economy along new and diverse lines. And for the task they could rely only on themselves.

They stumbled upon a novel, practical and democratic concept. The legislature authorized the formation of public utility districts having the right to own land and to exercise eminent domain. The PUDs were authorized to sell revenue bonds, generate and sell electricity and devote the proceeds of such sales to public purposes. A PUD could consist of a part of a county or of a number of counties.

In 1960 Chelan County, Washington, contained some 40,000 inhabitants. Since the Chelan County Public Utility District was established thirty-five years ago, it has sold more than $400 million worth of bonds and invested the money in hydro-electric dams and generators. It now owes $352 million, having retired the balance through its sinking fund. Total power sales amount to $30 million per year. More than a million dollars out of such income is contributed annually to finance schools, hospitals, libraries, land reclamation, reforestation and other essential public facilities and services. Abundant cheap power has attracted new industry. Good schools, a growing economy and a pleasant environment are drawing people into a county once threatened with wholesale abandonment. A "depressed area" has become a land of opportunity and growth.

A similar transformation has occurred in neighboring Grant County. That county had 42,000 inhabitants in 1960 and its income from electric power sales exceeded $20 million last year. The Grant County PUD is investing impressive sums in the development of plant sites and other facilities designed to spawn new economic muscle.

Appalachian states should emulate Washington by enacting similar enabling laws and organizing PUDs with boards appointed by the appropriate governor or elected by local inhabitants. Since a single county in Washington has sold $400 million worth of tax free debentures, a huge territory in Appalachia ought to be able to raise by the same method three or four billion dollars for regional rehabilitation.

An Appalachian PUD would formulate an over-all development plan—a program involving land, water, scenery, minerals, timber and people. It would build huge dams at strategic locations and create a vast complex of lakes. The lakes would generate hydro-electric power and provide cooling water for thermal generators. Most of the power would be fed into the growing national electric power grid for transmission to urban load centers. A part of the profits from power sales would be used for bond retirement and the balance would finance long-deferred public facilities and services, including schools, colleges, hospitals, health centers, libraries, land reclamation and sewage plants.

The local PUDs would purchase (by condemnation if necessary) the holdings of many of the absentee corporations. These minerals would be leased for mining, with guarantees written into the contracts for protection of the land and streams. Strip-mining would be prohibited except in those limited areas where total restoration of the land could be assured. Royalties would go into the treasury and substantial sums would be invested in watershed development, riding trails, camp sites and other facilities designed to convert the land into a recreation area.

The concept could be expanded beyond anything contemplated thus far. The idea of interstate compacts is an intriguing one. Such compacts have met with varying degrees of success and have often been stymied by ultra-conservative policies in the state houses. But the states are close to the people and, when wisely led, can act more effectively and precisely than the federal government.

The people of western Maryland, West Virginia, eastern Tennessee, eastern Kentucky, northern Alabama, western Virginia and western Pennsylvania share many similar problems and afflictions. All suffer in varying degrees from worn-out lands, dwindling populations and absentee ownership. All are mountainous and all have important mineral deposits. By compact the states could create an Appalachian Mountain Authority to accomplish on an interstate basis the things I have outlined for local PUDs.

The territory of the Appalachian Mountain Authority would be as big as that of the TVA. Its power to raise money would be vast. Its opportunities for service to the nation would be immeasurable.

Such an interstate authority could return the mineral wealth to the people without doing an injustice to the present owners. It could put the immense profits now flowing out of the region to work within the mountains. It could educate the highland people to a level equal to that enjoyed by America's most fortunate communities.

And it could demonstrate to the ranchers and Indians of the coal-rich Western states that if their lands are to be ransacked for fuel, the profits don't necessarily have to go to Wall Street. There are alternatives, and the profits could flow into Western improvements and Western pockets.

James Branscome

No one has done more to hold Appalachian life up for national ridicule than the producers of the "Beverly Hillbillies," "Green Acres" and "Hee Haw." It is no surprise, therefore, to find this brochure being handed out to tourists flocking into the Great Smokies through Asheville, North Carolina, airport:

"Hello! I'm Eddie Albert...and I want to personally invite you to see my new film about the 'un-City'....Connestee Falls. As you may know, I have been involved in the fight for the preservation of our environment for many years. I am proud to be associated with Realtec Incorporated, the developers of Connestee Falls, because here in the Blue Ridge Mountains of North Carolina, Realtec is creating an Un-City: uncrowded, unhurried, unpolluted.

"I sincerely want you to see my film about this remarkable environmental achievement.

Signed: Eddie Albert

Star of 'Green Acres.' "

Connestee Falls, and dozens of new developments like it in the North Carolina Blue Ridge, may be an eerie "Un-City" to Eddie Albert, but to the farmers of the mountains, it is an intrusion, the kind of intrusion that has driven the price of marginal farm and timber land from $100 an acre to a whopping $1,000 an acre in a half decade. So high has the price and taxation on mountain land become in the last few years that the dream of a mountain farmer to have at least one son stay home to till the soil has changed to the nightmare that he may not even be able to maintain the farm for his own retirement.

Sons and daughters of small, subsistence farmers along the Blue Ridge Parkway in Carroll County, Virginia, have been returning home lately to learn that the Groundhog Mountain Developers Corporation, a firm that sells lots to professional people from North Carolina cities, has used high-pressure tactics to force their parents to sell their land to them. According to Larry Bowman, a law student at Wake Forest and a native of the area, "These old folks—many of whom can't read or write—believe that they are only leasing, not selling, their land to these corporations. Others are so poor that the promise of a new roof or some worthless gratuity is traded for a small-print contract that in effect amounts to the theft of the land."

Only a few miles further down the Blue Ridge Parkway in Carroll County—the county that Mike Seeger says "has best preserved all those things that make up the Appalachian culture"—another firm is building a ski resort. The headline in the *Carroll News* on December 8, 1972, proclaimed, "Cascade Mountain—New Way of Life," and continued, "First there was Beech, then Sugar, and now Cascade. Yes, Cascade Mountain Resort will have one of the finest ski slopes in southwestern Virginia." As one of its many features the ski resort will have an "Olympic Village" with a lodge and motel named "Liebenschuen." And, of course, there will also be a country store. Carroll County needs a ski resort like San Francisco needs skyscrapers.

Thanks to these kinds of developments, the price of farmland is far beyond the means of farmers to buy it. An eighty-acre farm in Carroll, for example, was recently offered for public auction—something that mountaineers have traditionally done when there are several heirs to a farm and the community is in need of a social event. The hope has always been that one of the family or a close neighbor would "buy the old homeplace." This farm was privately offered by the heirs to a local man for $7,500, a figure that he considered excessive and rejected. At the public auction, flooded by land speculators and professionals from North Carolina in search of a "second home," the farm brought $20,000. A few weeks later one half of it was subdivided and sold for $40,000—$40,000 for a hillside that once grossed only a crop of wheat sufficient for the family's bread, pasture for four cows for the family's milk and a few cord of pulpwood to be sold to "put the kids in school" for the winter.

Carl Salmons, a small dairy farmer whose farm borders on the one mentioned above, says, "These people from North Carolina now own land on all four sides of me. I guess I'm next." The Salmons family is one of four families in the same hollow who have not sold out. Land speculation, urban affluence and overcrowding and the decline of small farmers has led to a situation where the right to be a hollow dweller—as most mountaineers have been for centuries and want to be now—carries with it the attendant obligation to be rich, an obligation that few mountaineers can meet.

Hundreds of proposals have been put forward in the past few

years to revitalize the rural economy. Cooperatives, rural loan banks and other kinds of palliatives have been advocated. All have failed to halt the stream of migration north. If Appalachia as a rural area is to survive, then more dramatic steps such as the following have to be taken:

(1) Corporate farming nationally must be stopped. It is a monopoly which allows high prices to be charged for inferior food.

(2) A regional producing and marketing system must be adopted which would forbid importing any food to Appalachia that could be grown locally by mountain farmers. This would entail the creation of a kind of Appalachian state, similar to a country of the European Common Market, which would protect mountain farmers at the expense of corporate farmers in Idaho and Colorado. Without doubt, the food produced under such a system would be cheaper, of higher quality and result in a rejuvenation of the region's economy.

(3) Land reform must be instituted. The giant holdings of corporations in Appalachia should be federalized and homesteaded the way the U.S. government seized and homesteaded the West. If we can do this to the poor Indians, there is no reason why we cannot do it to the rich corporations. This would simply be returning to the mountaineers the timber and land that they were swindled out of at the turn of the century. With this land, small family farms could again flourish in the mountains. Each homesteader would be required to sign a pledge that he would preserve his land for the next generation, and not allow it to be stripped or destroyed.

(4) Resort complexes that serve only middle-class skiers and other kinds of intruders should be prohibited. They bring only high land prices and disrespect for mountaineers. Either mountaineers stop this trend of exploitation, or there will be no native mountaineers left in a few years. Folks migrating to Northern cities know that mountaineers are not welcome in the rich suburbs, so there is no reason for us to make the suburbanites welcome in the mountains. There should be a regional law or gentlemen's understanding that mountaineers sell their land to each other, preserve it for their children, and never sell it to outsiders except when no other buyer can be found.

The South

In the South, the big land owners are timber companies and large plantations. Blacks never did own much land and are steadily losing what little they do own. In the following article, Robert S. Browne, director of the Black Economic Research Center, tells about the black loss of land in the South and suggests a possible remedy. The article was originally published by the Center for Community Economic Development, Cambridge, Massachusetts.

Robert S. Browne

For blacks in the South, the problem of land acquisition has been second only to the problem of land retention.

In the years following the Emancipation Proclamation, black people received title to a not insignificant portion of land in the South as bequests from former slave-masters or as inheritances via illegitimate unions which were for one reason or another publicly admitted to. These black landowners tended to be uneducated and totally ignorant of the legal intricacies involved in property ownership. Given the growing hostility toward blacks in the South from 1877 onward, it is not surprising that these simple black folk had great difficulty holding on to whatever land they had. There were no black lawyers or black real estate agents to protect their interests, and for the civil authorities to connive with their white compatriots at the expense of blacks was the rule rather than the exception.

In 1910, blacks were operating 890,000 farms in the South. Of these, 218,000 were fully or partially owned, while the rest were operated by tenants. In all, blacks managed to become full or part owners of 15 million acres of Southern land by 1910 without benefit of the Homestead Act and in the face of great hostility and violence.

But that was the peak. By 1950, black land ownership had declined to 12 million acres, and in 1969 it was down to 5.5 million acres, a drop of 54 percent in twenty years. It is probably accurate to say that white people own more of North America today than at any time in history, and this percentage continues to rise. Meanwhile, black Americans, whose stake in the United States is tenuous at best, are rapidly losing title to what little land they do have.

The blacks' loss of land in the South has coincided with the steady Northward migration. Unfortunately, the decision to migrate has not always proved to be a route to a better life. Whereas the migration of blacks to the urban North during World War II was largely inspired by the availability of well-paying jobs, the migration of the Fifties and Sixties derived primarily from the mechanization of Southern agriculture, especially the machine harvesting of cotton and corn. This time the Northern economies were unable to absorb the flood of unskilled immigrants, largely because the demand for unskilled industrial labor was being reduced by automation in industry. The result was a rapid growth of slums and the emergence of what is euphemistically termed "the urban crisis."

Any effective attack on the urban problem cannot ignore the roots of that problem, which is to say, it must attempt to deal with the poverty of black people in the rural South. There are a number of fronts upon which this poverty must be attacked. One is that of assuring that existing governmental programs are genuinely placed at the disposition of black people. Bitter experience has demonstrated how difficult it is to achieve this in the Southern states. Racial discrimination is merely a major but by no means the sole problem. Another is that many of the programs—for example, the Bank for Cooperatives and its sister institutions—are designed to help the solvent farmer. They cannot deal meaningfully with the problems of the very poor, be they black or white. These very poor people have no credit standing, no assets, often very little in the way of skills. Thus, they usually fail to meet the minimum qualification for participation in existing programs.

What the area urgently requires is an institution, or series of institutions which would have as an objective the creating of economically viable family units whose labor power, however unskilled, would be building equity for them. It is of the utmost importance that the descendants of slaves, these families which have never owned anything of substance since their arrival in North America, be afforded a means to acquire some minimal amount of wealth and to enjoy a modest degree of security. A legacy of dependence, whether on plantation masters or on federal doles, is not a sound basis for self-respect.

Specifically, what is needed is a new institution dedicated to the goals of: (a) transfering land to poor, especially black, rural people; (b) facilitating the improvement of this land through the provision of housing, water, and the like; and (c) developing profitable employment opportunities on this land. Without specifying what the final design of such an institution might be, the following broad outline may be suggestive.

One possible approach is an institution which would collectively own land on behalf of those who live on it. The community institution in which title was vested would lease land on a long-term basis to those who lived on it. Improvements could be made by both the community and the individual; in the latter case, title to the improvement would rest in the dweller and could be sold by him to the community should he move off the land.

Collective ownership is, of course, not a *sine qua non* for a large-scale transference of land to poor black folk. It can be done on a straight private ownership basis, but with some "title protection" built in. Presumably, plots would be contiguous so that opportunities for cooperative efforts would be available.

At least two types of financial provisions would be required to realize such a land reform effort: a mortgage plan and an equity plan. Some governmental agency would need to guarantee the mortgage on the land. It would also have to provide the equity portion of the transaction, in the form of a long-term or deferred payment, interest-free second mortgage loan. Additionally, it would have to subsidize the interest rate on the first mortgage.

Families on welfare should not be excluded from the program. Rather, inasmuch as their meager stipends must cover a rental payment to someone, how much better to permit this payment to be used to purchase some equity in a piece of real property!

An alternative approach would be to revive the concept of the Homestead Act, from which black people obtained so little benefit. Many blacks feel that the government should give them land just as it gave land to white settlers. There are, of course, limitations to such a proposal, since most of the remaining public land is not suitable for human habitation, or is located where black people do not live. Nevertheless, there are publicly owned parcels scattered throughout the South which would be suited for homesteading. The Departments of Defense and Interior are both large title-holders to such land, as are other departments to a lesser degree.

In addition to transferring land, the new institution should help develop income-producing programs which would enable new landowners to sustain economically viable family units. In some cases this will mean truck farming; sometimes it may mean large-scale cultivation on a cooperative basis; elsewhere it can mean that processing facilities, or perhaps some industrial opportunity, will be developed, perhaps with a government subsidy during an initial period. Since such a subsidy would be largely in lieu of a welfare payment, it might very well be an economical way of dealing with rural poverty. It is certainly likely to be cheaper than continued out-migration with its incalculable costs in terms of urban and human deterioration.

The Northern Plains

*In the Northern Plains states—Montana, Wyoming and the
Dakotas—the largest land owners, besides the government and several
Indian tribes, are railroads, energy companies and resort developers, many
of whom overlap. Dorothy Bradley, a Montana state representative,
provides some general background on land problems in the region,
especially railroad ownership, and William L. Bryan Jr., an environ-
mentalist with the Northern Rockies Action Group, discusses the impact
of the great Western coal rush on the Northern Cheyenne and Crow
Indians. Both papers were originally presented at the First National
Conference on Land Reform.*

————————————————————— Dorothy Bradley

In the latter half of the 19th Century, two major events
occurred which had far-reaching effects on future land use in the
Northern Plains. First, the Homestead Act brought barbed wire
and steel plows to the virgin grasslands, and many new people
who were not familiar with the semi-arid prairies. Second, the
building of the railroads brought more development and also
control of vast amounts of land by the railroads. In Montana
alone, the Northern Pacific received almost 15 million acres, or
16 percent of the total area.

Unfortunately, the small allotments granted under the
Homestead Act were not designed for economic operations on
semi-arid lands. More attention was given to farming than grazing
until the Stock Raising Homestead Act of 1916, which allowed up
to 640 acres for livestock purposes, but even this was insufficient.
The error of the homestead policy for the Northern Plains was not
fully realized until the drought of the 1930s, which caused mass
abandonment of homesteads. A fairly steady de-ruralization has
continued since that time. Small subsistence farms have been
replaced by larger commercial operations and more land has
been committed to grazing. Approximately 45 percent of
Montana is presently ranchland.

The Indians of Montana received 46 million acres of reservation land—approximately half the state—but the supposed generosity was short-lived. Through years of inappropriate policies, allotment acts and ceding of lands, this acreage dwindled to about 5.5 million acres, much of it barren and of little value except for the new interest that Consol, Shell and other energy companies have shown in the coal which underlies it.

This history points out mistakes which we cannot afford to repeat. We have learned that small agricultural units arbitrarily limited to 160 acres are not necessarily a viable way of life in the dry plains. We have also learned the dangers of absentee corporate ownership.

The Burlington Northern railroad, heir to the Northern Pacific, still owns 2.4 million acres in eleven states, and has mineral rights on another 6 million acres. In Montana alone, the BN controls about one-tenth of all private land. Serious forest management problems arise because of the alternate BN sections interspersed with National Forest lands. Additionally, problems are occurring in eastern Montana because of BN's control and development interest in vast amounts of coal.

Another problem involves BN land next to the Big Sky Corporation, a huge resort development. The Big Sky situation has serious implications for efforts to classify the adjacent Spanish Peaks as wilderness. A sizeable tract of elk winter range and non-alpine wilderness could be added to the Spanish Peaks wilderness area. However, because it contains 22 sections of BN holdings, the Forest Service deleted this critical area from its wilderness proposal, thus cutting the total acreage in half.

What are possible solutions to these problems?

Regarding wilderness classification, Congress can authorize the acquisition of private lands under the Wilderness Act of 1964. In addition it is high time to think in terms of condemning land for the public as wilderness, while of course giving just compensation for the land taken. For BN lands, an appropriate compensation might be $2.50 an acre.

A local group in the Spanish Peaks vicinity offered another more original solution. Noting that land was given to the railroad 100 years ago to help pay original construction costs, noting also that the public gives millions of dollars each year to AMTRAK, and noting further that proposed legislation would use tax money to build box cars for railroads to move agricultural products, the group suggested that a fair value be placed on each section of BN land and when a subsidy is given to the railroad, that value of land should revert to public ownership.

An immediate problem is that of coal development. The immensity of the problem is partly due to the increasing demand for low sulfur coal, and partly to the fact that BN holds mineral rights on many more acres than it holds surface rights. The most recent figures show that over three-fourths of the coal leases are on private land, and of those private leases, half are BN's. More specifically, the total acreage leased in Montana is 730,000 acres. The picture is a rosy one for BN since it is not only making money from the leased coal, but also by shipping it. Revenue to BN in 1971 from coal hauling was $69 million, and is expected to double in five years.

A good initial approach would be enforcing the 1906 Hepburn Railroad Act which prohibits railroads from transporting commodities in which they have an interest.

Lest one think that these proposals are harsh, it should be remembered that BN has long enjoyed favored tax status on its holdings. Sanders County Commissioner Wesley Stearns has stated that BN pays only three cents an acre on its forest holdings in the rich Thompson River country. "Under present taxation schedules," he says, "I pay more property taxes on my home than BN does on 10,000 acres of timber lands."

—————————————————————*William L. Bryan, Jr.*

Over 40 percent of the nation's coal reserves are in the Northern Plains. The coal is easy to mine, with an average of 20 to 100 feet of overburden. It lies in seams up to 257 feet thick, and is very low in sulfur.

The North Central Power Study declared open season on this resource in 1971. The study was done by the Bureau of Reclamation and 36 utilities. Although its recommendations aren't being implemented at present, an undeclared black gold rush is in high gear. There is absolutely no thought being given to planned development, as each energy company tries to grab as much coal as possible. In Montana alone, 1.3 million acres have come under some form of corporate control. The list of companies involved reads like a Who's Who of the energy industry: Peabody, Chevron, Consol, Shell, Gulf, Westmoreland, Kerr McGee, F.M.C., American Metals Climax (Amax), Pacific Power and Light, U.S. Steel, Mobil. They are all there and thriving.

Sadly, the rise in absentee control through prospecting permits, mineral leases and outright land purchase is continuing at a rapid rate. One reason is that so much of the coal is federally owned. A recent study of 900,000 acres in Montana found that, while 65 percent of the surface is privately owned, only 7 percent of the coal is privately held. Until 1973, a company that leased the coal rights could bring condemnation proceedings against the surface owner. This incredible law was repealed, but court battles are certain to follow.

The most obscene exploitation of people and land by energy companies is occurring on the reservations of the Crow and Northern Cheyenne Indians. These reservations lie in the heart of the coal fields and fortunately, the mineral rights are owned by the respective tribes. However, on the Northern Cheyenne reservations of 437,000 acres, over 240,000 acres are held under lease and exploratory permit by coal companies. That amounts to 55 percent of the reservation under some type of control by Peabody, Consol, Amax and Chevron.

On the Crow reservation, 292,680 acres are under exploratory permits and outright leases. Gulf, Shell, Westmoreland, Peabody and Amax are the absentee Crow land controllers and each are talking of gasification plants for their coal. Gulf is also talking of a planned community on the reservation for upwards of 200,000 people.

At first the energy companies worked on the Northern Cheyennes in such a way that virtually no tribal members knew what was happening. Eventually, the Northern Cheyennes began to see the ominous future that was in store. In 1972 the Northern Cheyenne Landowners Association was formed; it began to publicize what the absentee coal companies were up to. The Tribal Council did an about-face and formally petitioned the Department of Interior to declare null and void all the coal permits and leases on the reservation. Thus far, the Interior has not acceded to the request, so the Northern Cheyennes will now have to sue.

The stakes are high for both sides. The energy industry stands to make billions of dollars; for the Cheyennes, it is a fight for their land, culture and very existence.

The Midwest

A popular notion is that the Midwest is characterized by small, family-owned and operated farms. This is only partly true, and is becoming less so as time passes. Research by Paul Wallace Gates has shown that in Kansas and Nebraska, 28 and 24 percent respectively of the farms were tenant-operated by 1890. Now, two recent studies in these same states show that absentee ownership is increasing.

The first study, by the Center for Rural Affairs, Walthill, Nebraska, was presented at the First Midwest Land Conference held in Cedar Rapids, Iowa, in November 1973. The second, by Kemp Houck, is based on extensive research conducted by the Kansas Farm Project, Lawrence, Kansas.

Center for Rural Affairs

This study examines the extent of large farm units, land ownership by non-family corporations and the amount of professional farm management in northeast Nebraska.

Data was gathered from county assessor, treasurer and clerk offices. Occupation tax reports filed in the Secretary of State's office were used to determine the classification of corporations.

The findings indicate that:

—Large farm units are rarely owned wholly by the operator. In the eight counties for which data is available, the percentage of land in large operating units which is leased by the operator ranges from 33 to 90 percent.

—Non-family corporate ownership of agricultural land in the study area is not extensive in terms of the number of acres currently owned, but its growth in recent years is remarkable. Nearly 65 percent of land currently owned by such corporations was acquired within the past five years.

—More than a third of the corporations owning agricultural land are not authorized to do business in Nebraska. These

48

corporations have actively acquired land in the past five years.

—The professional farm management business is concentrated among a very few urban-based firms. The top four companies have nearly 72 percent of the land management business (measured in acres), and the top two companies enjoyed almost 60 percent. The largest company manages 61,267 acres over the area studied, amounting to 45 percent of all the land managed.

These findings are disturbing to those who believe that agriculture should be controlled by people who live and work on the land. They reinforce the notion that agriculture is becoming structurally specialized—that ownership, operation and management of land will be separated functions. If this trend continues, it is possible to forecast the development of a Corn Belt class structure rigidly defined along owner-manager-worker lines.

The degree of concentration in the professional management sector is already pronounced. By any standards, monopoly conditions exist in this business within the area studied.

The data on corporate ownership is less alarming but just as definitive. Much of the land owned by non-family farm corporations belongs to companies which trace their origin to the 19th Century. These companies, dominated by the Brown Land Company, are all apparently tied to the Brown-Ives-Goddard families which carried the tradition of the English gentry into Rhode Island, and from there to the Midwest. This group, which we call the Rhode Island group, is historically associated with the Browns of Brown University, and is active in several areas of Nebraska. In 1972, the Brown Land Company received a $23,182 direct crop payment from the USDA for set-aside acreage in Burt County. Brown's holdings in other areas of Nebraska are known to include ranches in the sandhills and a 7,500-acre irrigated corn farm in Holt County. The principal in the Brown Land Company is John Nicholas Brown of Rhode Island. He is also a director of the LeDioyt Land Company, the second largest professional farm management firm in the study area. LeDioyt manages much if not all of the Brown holdings.

The failure of a sizeable number of land-owning corporations—including the Brown Land Company—to file or keep current necessary papers with the Secretary of State is an important discovery. Beyond the fact that these corporations have escaped paying an occupation tax lies the troublesome fact that their maverick behavior prevents the public from knowing who and what they are. Information is available only to the most diligent researcher who is willing to spend long hours in county court houses. This is an inordinate amount of effort for basic public information.

Kemp Houck

This report on land tenure in Kansas is based on a survey of the county plats (land ownership maps) of each of the 105 counties in the state. We counted 28 corporations and 164 individuals, families, partnerships, estates or trusts which own more than 5,000 acres in 55 counties of the state. Of these, 67 own more than 10,000 acres, and four own more than 50,000 acres. There are a number of serious limitations in these results, however.

First, we generally found the county maps to be about five years out of date. Since land in Kansas is being bought and sold at the rate of 40,000 transactions a year, and since the current trend is toward larger farms and inflated land prices, it is reasonable to expect that an updated picture would show heavier concentrations of ownership.

Second, county plats list principal owners only. They provide no information on land rental, land management or limited partnerships with "straw" owners. Farmers are often aware that several thousand acres have been bought in their neighborhood in the name of someone who does not live in the county. Not knowing the name of the owner leaves a number of questions unanswered for the community: How heavily will they be spraying? How deep will they be drilling irrigation wells?

Finally, we did not attempt to compile figures on federal, state or institutional ownership, which is considerable. Especially in the southeastern corner and in the northern tier of counties, there is a significant pattern of quarter sections held by banks, insurance companies and the Federal Land Bank. This pattern has an obvious relation to the depressed economic state of these areas.

The major concentrations in Kansas are in the westernmost counties and in the Flint Hills area. Many factors lie behind this concentration, one being that, with increased agricultural industrialization, it has been possible (whether it is necessary is another question) to produce grains and sorghums and to manage pasture on a very large scale.

Another factor is that, with some western counties having more than 100,000 acres under irrigation by systems capable of drawing more than 1,000 gallons of ground water per minute, the competition for water has added to the demand for land adjacent to lakes and rivers.

History is another factor. The ceding of Indian lands, combined with the subsequent granting of one-sixth of the state in forty mile rights-of-way to railroads, brought on a scramble for land which caused Horace Greeley to remark about Kansas: "As to the infernal spirit of land speculation and monopoly, I think no state ever suffered from it more severely than this." Intended to encourage homesteading, the checkerboard pattern of odd-numbered alternating sections owned by the federal government laid the ground for large land holdings such as the Scully property (57,790 acres in Marion County).

Most Kansas counties reached their peak population during the golden age of American agriculture, 1911-1914. After that, the general decline was accelerated by the Depression and Dust Bowl, wars and shifts in international trade. With each population loss came a new aggregation of large holdings.

During the 1960s, 65 rural counties in Kansas suffered an outmigration of more than 30 percent of their male youth. Kansas is now number two among the states in number of counties with more than 20 percent of their population being over 65. Land policies decided in the 1970s will inevitably determine future vintages of the grapes of wrath.

New England

In northern New England, the dominant land owners have long been the paper and pulp companies. But, as Geoffrey Faux points out, some new land barons are moving in: conglomerates, developers, speculators and energy companies.

Faux is a former director of economic development programs at the Office of Economic Opportunity. He now works with the Exploratory Project for Economic Alternatives and lives on a 60-acre blueberry farm in Whitefield, Maine. The following selection is taken from his remarks at the First National Conference on Land Reform.

————————————————————————Geoffrey Faux

Almost 200 years ago the people of northern New England revolted against an absentee landowner, George III. We have all been taught that that particular land reform was successful. But look hard and you will see that after 200 years we have simply traded one set of absentee owners for another. The new aristocrats have names like International Paper, Scott Paper, IT&T, Gulf and Western, Chase Manhattan, Merrill Lynch, Pierce, Fenner and Smith.

They don't tell us very much about their holdings, but what we do know gives a hint of how much of a colony northern New England is. In Vermont 19 out of the 22 firms employing more than 500 people are headquartered out of state. In New Hampshire 16 out of 20 are headquartered out of state. In Maine 32 of 43, almost 75 percent of all firms employing more than 500, are headquartered out of state.

These are low estimates. Many firms headquartered in these states are owned by outsiders, including the power companies, railroads and financial institutions.

And of course there is the land. Recent estimates put the percentage of absentee ownership as high as 80 percent of the state of Maine. A dozen pulp and timber companies own 52 percent of the state. They buy and sell whole townships like kids playing monopoly. Among the losers are the men who cut pulp in the woods; the price the monopolists pay for wood pulp is about the same that it was twenty years ago.

And things are getting worse. The demand for recreation land has spurred developers to overrun Vermont, New Hampshire and Maine. Along the coast, large energy companies are moving in on natural deep water harbors to build their refineries. The economic development that the corporations boast of provides few jobs for local people. For example, it takes only a handful of people to run an oil refinery. But one oil spill can completely destroy the clam, lobster and fishing beds from which thousands of New Englanders make their living.

As in most places, the family farm in our region is rapidly becoming a curiosity. New England is not generally good farming country, but even in the crops we can grow to advantage, like potatoes, and blueberries, and in the fishing industry, the corporations are taking over.

In recent years northern New England has become a tourist and retirement mecca. People from the cities of the Northeast corridor have flocked to Maine, Vermont and New Hampshire to escape congestion, overcrowding and pollution. Between 1964 and 1969 spending by tourists almost doubled and it has continued to rise since. Tourism is now the number one industry in the area, and prices have skyrocketed as a result. Land that sold for $20 an acre in 1961 cannot be had for less than $200 today. Stories abound of how land speculators and wealthy people from Boston and New York bought land dirt cheap from poor farmers a few years ago and have made fortunes on the increase in value.

The effect of this on the poor is profound. Where previously people could pretty much get by with a garden, by hunting and fishing and by digging clams, the rise in taxes, rents and the general cost of living is squeezing them mercilessly. And the land itself, which used to be open for hunting and fishing, is now being fenced off for the pleasure of outsiders. Out of 1800 miles of coastline in Maine, only thirteen are open to the public.

Gradually the poor rural New Englander is being driven out of his community, forced into Boston, Hartford, Providence, or the sparsely settled backwoods areas, where opportunities are practically nil. It reminds one of the cycle of uprooting and resettlement that destroyed the native American Indian during the 19th Century.

The tragedy is that tourism and recreation is the most important force to hit northern New England in a century. It could open up all kinds of opportunities for the underemployed, especially now that recreation has become a four-season activity.

But the poor can't get a handle on these opportunities because they are controlled by out-of-staters in the context of rampant disregard for the indigenous population.

It's not that we in New England have not been trying to change the situation. We have tried all the conventional solutions—land use regulation, planning, zoning and other controls. But none of these work very well. The lure of profits from land speculation and the weight of corporate power have defeated all our reasonable, liberal efforts.

Some efforts, like zoning which consistently benefits the large landowner with capital and political power, have made things worse. We also are beginning to tax farmland at present, rather than highest use. But that seems to be doing more for the speculators than for the farmers.

If land use planning, regulation, zoning and lower tax assessments are not the answer, what is? I don't have a magic formula. But I do have some general notions on land reform that I would like to share with you.

For openers, it is clear that we have to stop encouraging absentee land ownership and speculation by closing the tax loopholes that subsidize this kind of non-productive activity.

Second, we have to actively discourage large landholdings through tax policies that work against size perhaps, for example, through progressive property taxes with exemptions for homesteads and small land holdings.

Third, we should levy heavy if not confiscatory taxes on large capital gains arising from land speculation. It makes no economic sense to permit huge profits from the ownership of land the value of which rises through no effort on the part of the owner.

Fourth, we should stop thinking only in terms of controls and start examining what is really meant by private land ownership.

My point is reflected in the story of the hobo who was found sleeping on a rich man's lawn one morning. "See here," shouted the rich man out of his window. "You will have to get out of here. This is my land."

"Oh, where did you get it?" asked the hobo.

"My father gave it to me," replied the rich man.

"And where did he get it?" asked the hobo.

"From his father," said the rich man.

"And where did his father get it?" asked the hobo.

"Why, he fought the Indians for it," said the rich man proudly.

"O.K." said the hobo. "Come on down here and I'll fight you for it right now."

We in New England are beginning to fight. Maine saw its first state-wide land reform conference in 1973. Represented were farmers, woodcutters, fishermen, environmentalists and a variety of Maine people.

Up in Aroostook County, where we grow rocks and potatoes—in that order—a large out-of-state corporation recently bought up a number of small potato processing plants. Its first acts were to lay off some workers and to cut the price it offered farmers for potatoes. The workers struck the plant and the farmers organized a boycott. Workers and farmers have not had much of an alliance in the past, but now for perhaps the first time they are seeing a common enemy and they have begun to talk to each other.

It's only a beginning, but we feel good about it.

Indian Lands

The Indian land problem is not confined to a single region. Rather, it stems from a long and tragic history of conquest and destruction that began on the Atlantic shores and still goes on—albeit with less bloodshed—today. The latest rush for Indian lands and water rights is occurring in places like Arizona and Montana, where energy companies are eager to develop coal that lies beneath Indian reservations.

White people have never understood the Indian concept of the sacredness and non-divisibility of land; just compare our stewardship of the North American continent during the past 200 years with the Indian stewardship over the preceeding 1,000 years! Of course, it is too late to get white men out of North America, but there is at least a chance for a more enlightened policy toward Indians. Here Kirke Kickingbird and Karen Ducheneaux survey the origins of U.S. policy toward native Americans and recommend a new policy based on establishing an inviolable Indian land base.

Kickingbird, a Kiowa, is an attorney with the Institute for Development of Indian Law in Washington. Ducheneaux, a Cheyenne River Sioux, is a staff writer for the American Indian Press Association. The following excerpt is taken from their book, One Hundred Million Acres *[Macmillan, 1973].*

——Kirke Kickingbird and Karen Ducheneaux

The major source of all Indian-white conflict and confrontation has been land.

When Indians fought for their land, their struggles were called uprisings, their victories recorded as massacres. Because whites could not understand the Indians' concept of land tenure, they derided the communal use of land as inefficient or, worse, thought that the Indians were trying to "get away with something." This attitude developed in the remote past and has characterized the relationship between Indians and whites to this day.

The world of the European prior to the discovery of the New

World was relatively simple. It was flat, finite and Christian. The discovery of the Western Hemisphere was a shock to most Europeans. No one had expected to find two immense continents sitting out there where the edge of the flat earth should have been.

In order to encourage exploration, the doctrine was developed that the European nation that discovered a land had exclusive rights to trade with it. This doctrine encouraged a dramatic race between exploring expeditions to "claim" lands on behalf of their respective sovereigns. It was not long before Europeans decided that their nations should not claim only trading privileges in an area but the land itself.

There was a major flaw in the doctrine of discovery: no provision was ever made for the natives of the "newly discovered" lands to obtain a final decision on their titles. Once the riches of the New World began to pour into the coffers of Europe, any consideration of native land tenure was conveniently put to rest in favor of absolute rule by the conquering power.

After the Revolution, American political theorists contended that the United States had stepped into the shoes of England with respect to the doctrine of discovery.

The United States claimed the right to extinguish all Indian titles to lands on the continent within its domestic borders, and the Indian tribes were deprived of any right of appeal. It became merely a matter of when, not if, the United States would take the lands. The assumption upon which this policy was based was that land title could only be acquired from the federal government. Indian titles were considered nonexistent.

The earliest policy on Indian lands envisioned the gradual removal of the eastern tribes to the stark plains of the West, where it was thought that no white man could exist. The policy was a step above genocide. The savagery of the Indian, his obvious inability to use the land according to Christian principles of commerce, and his persistence in his pagan religions were used to justify his banishment to the great American desert, as the Great Plains were then called. Indian land policy was thus shifted from one of original ownership to allocation by relative levels of civilization, a wholly cultural conception lacking any legal basis whatsoever.

With the adoption of the Constitution, the colonies became a federal government in which functions were allocated to the various branches of government. The President, with the advice and consent of the Senate, could make treaties with the Indians that had the same legal status as those made with foreign nations. But treaties never gave the tribes a totally sovereign and independent status in the eyes of the United States because the doctrine of discovery lurked in the background.

The interstate commerce clause authorized Congress to make laws with respect to trading with Indian tribes and with foreign nations. The first laws passed by Congress concerning the Indians primarily involved trade. With constant pressure from Western settlers, Congress began to alter its duties from mere trade regulation to total control over every aspect of Indian programs and policies. The courts have accepted the presumption that Congress always acts with wisdom and in good faith when dealing with Indians. It is a fanciful notion rather than a fact of life.

As the role of the federal government in Indian affairs has grown, various agencies have come into being that deal with Indian lands. When the Bureau of Indian Affairs was transferred to the Department of the Interior in 1849, it was placed in competition with a number of the department's other agencies, all addressing themselves to the task of supervising national physical resources. For the most part these agencies have been devoted to the confiscation of Indian lands rather than to safeguarding them for their Indian owners. The 20th century has seen a rapid growth of policies devoted to the exploitation of Indian lands by government agencies, with the Interior Department supervising the rape of Indian legal rights in a most interesting manner.

Within the Interior Department, the Bureau of Reclamation and the Wildlife Service from their very inception have coveted Indian lands. These agencies, supported on the outside by powerful groups of citizens and commercial interests, have generally determined what position would be officially taken by the parent Interior Department as protector of Indian reservation lands and waters.

It would be fair to say that if a private trustee were discovered acting in the same manner as the Interior Department does toward the Indians, he would immediately be indicted for gross violation of his trust. In all but a few cases, bureaucrats in the department have deliberately thwarted attempts by the Indian tribes to keep their lands under tribal ownership.

A case in point: an effort to take away the water rights of a number of tribes on the Colorado River in Arizona and the Rio Grande in New Mexico was made in the courts in 1971. Indian tribes had been aware that they might lose their water rights, rights that were essential to their existence in the southwestern deserts.

A number of tribes made official appeals to the Justice and Interior Departments. In a letter to Minerva Jenkins, tribal chairwoman of the Fort Mojave Tribal Council, at Needles, California,

Solicitor General Erwin N. Griswold promised that the Justice Department would fully defend the rights of the tribe to water on the Colorado River. "Please be assured," he wrote in November 1970, "that the government intends to make the Supreme Court fully aware of its obligation as trustee of Indian water rights in this matter (the *Eagle River* case), and of any bearing that the decision may have on those rights." When, however, the Justice Department filed its brief in the case in which it was to assert the Indian water rights before the Supreme Court, it said in an obscure footnote, "To the best of our knowledge, none of the reserved water rights claimed by the United States in Water Division No. 5 relate to Indian lands."

The result of the *Eagle River* decision was to place all Indian water rights at the mercy of the court systems of the various states, courts that are notoriously anti-Indian. The tribes issued loud protests and finally a subcommittee of the Senate, headed by Senator Edward Kennedy, looked into the deprivation of water rights, concentrating on conflicts of interest within the Interior Department. Questioned by the committee, Harrison Loesch, assistant secretary of the Interior for land management, who oversees the administration of Indian programs, lamely related that he did not "know" that Indians placed a high priority on water.

The situation is far beyond the point of simple scandal. It is so blatant that even the President has been forced to concede the total abdication by federal officials of their responsibilities for the protection of Indian rights. In a special message on Indians sent to Congress in July 1970, President Nixon outlined new legislation of major proportions. He called for the creation of an Indian Trust Counsel Authority, a special agency independent of both the Justice and Interior Departments, to defend Indian rights. Indians have been urging this sort of thing for a long time.

Today, out of the vast continent once "owned" by American Indian people, slightly less than 100 million acres remain. Of this amount some 40 million acres only recently came into Indian hands through the Alaska land settlement, and groups of whites are now appealing that legislation in an attempt to reduce the Indian landholdings still further.

But the type of ownership that American Indians enjoy today is only theoretical. The federal government still holds Indian lands through the administrative structure of the assistant secretary of land management in the Department of the Interior. It is still accepted in the halls of Congress that Indians do not really own their lands but live on them at the pleasure of Congress. This anti-Indian sentiment is well understood everywhere in Indian country and is the major inhibiting force in developing Indian reservations.

We propose that the United States enter a new phase in its relationship with the American Indian by creating a new doctrine of Indian legal rights with respect to land titles and ownership. We propose a new category of legal status for Indian lands and a policy to stabilize the Indian land base at 100 million acres by restoring lands illegally taken during the last century. We believe this program should naturally be the first step in solving the problems of Indians created by the accidents and incidents of American history.

All lands in the new legal category called Indian lands would be held, as are all lands of Indians at present, in a legal status that makes them immune from state and federal taxation. Tribal governments would have complete control of zoning, hunting and fishing, gathering of berries, wild ricing, cutting of timber and mining of minerals. They could never be subjected to condemnation by state or local governments or by federal agencies for any purpose whatsoever. They would also have first-priority water rights on all streams arising on or passing through the lands, as they do now, but in any proposed use of water on any river or drainage system that would affect Indian rights to water, the full potential use of the Indian tribe would be determined prior to the determination of any other rights to the water.

Indian lands would not be subjected to the control of the Bureau of Indian Affairs or the Department of the Interior. They would be under the control of the tribe to which the lands belonged. Such lands could be sold by the tribe only after any plan to sell lands was presented to the whole membership of the tribe meeting in a general council and was discussed for a period of three consecutive years.

The termination of the Klamath Indians of Oregon, the Siletz and Grande Ronde Indians of Oregon, the Affiliated Utes of Utah and the bands of Paiutes of southern Utah would be ended. These tribes would be restored to full federal status, with their lands placed in the new category of Indian lands.

To facilitate the establishment of a permanent Indian land base, we recommend that two special funds be created for use by tribal governments. One fund of low-interest loans would be made available to Indian tribes to purchase allotments of individual Indians, the lands thus purchased to be added to the existing tribal estates. The other would be a no-interest fund for small tribes to purchase lands not now under Indian ownership for expansion of their existing tribal land base consistent with their needs.

We additionally recommend that the General Services Administration convene a general meeting and inform the Indian tribes about land currently surplus or soon to be surplus. We advocate priority be given to those Indian tribes or groups that present adequate use-plans for lands that are or may become surplus to federal needs.

All previous proposals for improving the condition of American Indian people have revolved around the confiscation of their lands and pious admonitions for them to stop being Indians. In the name of justice, mercy, sanity, common sense, fiscal responsibility and rationality we present this program to place Indian communities on a solid legal and economic basis once and for all. We appeal to the American people to demand of their Senators and Congressmen a new day for American Indian people, without any hidden agendas or any shifting of concepts and programs to confiscate Indian lands in the name of progress, patriotism or religion.

*As the homesteaders and the railroads moved in,
the Indians were rounded up,*

Bureau of Reclamation, National Archives.
*Homesteader turns the sod for the first
time: Montana, 1908.*

F. C. Wintemute, Library of Congress. *The pioneer days reenacted; Montana, 1908.*

Andrew J. Russell, The Oakland Museum. *Union Pacific bridging the Green River; Wyoming, 1868.*

Cheyennes and Arapahos do the Ghost Dance; Oklahoma Territory, 1889.

U.S. Signal Corps, National Archives. *Crow prisoners; Montana, 1887.*

U.S. Signal Corps., National Archives. *Cheyenne Indians; Montana, ca. 1884.*

U.S. Signal Corps., National Archives. *After the surrender; Fort Bowie, Arizona.*

Russell Lee, FSA. *Washington, 1941.*

...forests were mined, the minerals

                      stripped away.

Clarence S. Sinclair, USDA. *Clearcut, St. Joe National Forest; Idaho, 1966.*

USDA. *Pulpwood pile; Maine, 1948.*

T. L. Gettings. *Strip mine; Pennsylvania, 1974.*

John Collier, Jr., FSA. *Slag pile and company houses; Pennsylvania, 1942.*

Marion Post-Wolcott, FSA. *Coal miner's child taking home a can of kerosene; West Virginia, 1938.*

T. H. O'Sullivan, Library of Congress. *Slave family on J. J. Smith plantation; South Carolina, 1862.*

Dorothea Lange, FSA. *Hoe culture; Alabama, 1936.*

Ben Shahn, FSA.
Cotton pickers; Arkansas, 1935.

The poor were systematically exploited.

Eugene Suarez Sr., Bureau of Indian Affairs. *Indian village; Gila Bend Reservation, Arizona.*

Bureau of Indian Affairs. *Indian home; Rosebud Reservation, South Dakota, 1966.*

It is the same today as yesterday.

Ted Dietz, USDA. *Strip mine; North Dakota, 1968.*

Bob Fitch. *Mother, son, dog and hoe; Mississippi.*

Larry Rana, USDA. *Child of poverty; Maryland, 1969.*

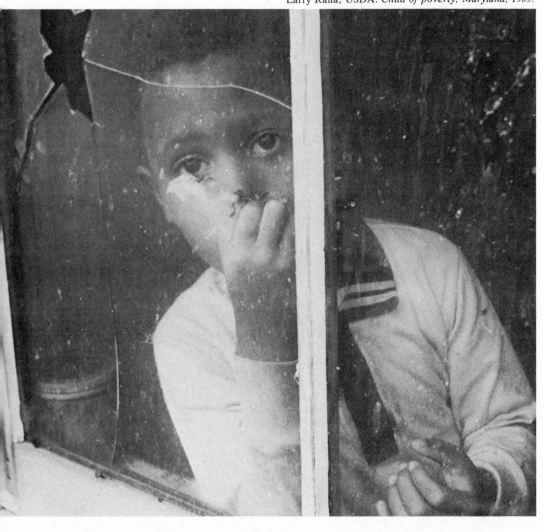

William H. Hylton. *North Carolina, 1967.*

James Punkre. *West Virginia, 1973.*

Part III
Food,
Farms and Technology

The Industrialization of Food

What happens when giant corporations take over the food production process "from seedling to supermarket?" For one thing, food costs more. For another, it doesn't taste as good. As director of the Agribusiness Accountability Project, Jim Hightower has closely studied the impact of corporations on food prices and food quality. Here, he reports on the industrialization of food and tells why urban consumers should join the fight for rural land reform.

Jim Hightower

Gwaltney Smithfield hams and sausages are packaged and advertised to give off a feeling of the old farm place and the unrushed process of a Virginia smokehouse. The reality is not nearly as down home as the image. Gwaltney is owned and managed by the world's biggest conglomerate, IT&T.

Country goodness, made the old-fashioned way, is the advertising pitch of Pepperidge Farm bakery products. The company is owned by the food conglomerate, Campbell Soup.

Is regional beer, brewed the local way, a source of enjoyment for you? Maybe a Burgermeister, a Hamms, a Waldech or a Buckhorn? They all are now a product of Heublein Inc., a Connecticut conglomerate.

The American food supply is increasingly concentrated, standardized and industrialized. The same factory techniques, the same market domination and the same selling gimmicks that Detroit brought to automobiles now are being applied to food. It is at least questionable that consumers really want to turn this corporate power loose in their pantries.

Before the family farmer is discarded, we ought to take a hard look at where we are being led. It is not just the family farm that is threatened by corporate agribusiness, it is the price and quality of the American food supply.

81

To consumers and family farmers alike, the most significant reality of modern agriculture is the concentration occurring in every phase of the food system. A few very powerful processing and marketing corporations are increasingly able to tie the entire food system together "from inputs through retailing," as USDA economist John Lee puts it. Tenneco—which not only makes farm machinery, chemicals, fuel and food containers, but also grows, packages, markets and retails food—has an appropriate slogan to sum up its pervasiveness: "Seedling to Supermarket." Del Monte Corporation assures consumers that it can take care of food needs "from womb to tomb."

Some corporations in a position to grow food, process it, package and ship it, wholesale and retail it, are even cooking it for you too. *Nation's Restaurant News*, a trade publication, counts more than 40 major food manufacturers and processors that now own restaurants. Pillsbury (Burger King), General Mills (Red Lobster Inn), Quaker Oats (Magic Pan), Campbell Soup (Jack-In-The-Box), General Foods (Burger Chef) and Green Giant (Henrici's) are just a few of the food middlemen with arms that reach all the way to the dining table.

In a concentrated corporate-controlled food system, prices do not go down, they go up. Competition is replaced by a new spirit of cooperation and coordination. As has happened in many manufacturing industries, agricultural efficiency will decline as market concentration enables food companies to pass on to consumers the cost of inefficiencies and excess profits.

The Federal Trade Commission found in a 1972 study that consumers are being overcharged more than $2 billion a year for food because of monopolies within just 13 food lines.

The added costs of concentration—such as burgeoning administrative staffs, increased advertising budgets and inflated management salaries—most certainly will be rung up on the consumer's tab at the checkout counter. It's doubtful that any savings from a concentrated food system will be passed along to shoppers. Del Monte Corporation, for example, recently abandoned its white asparagus operations in California, Oregon and Washington and moved those operations to Mexico, where cheap labor reduced the corporation's production costs by 45 percent. But the price of Del Monte asparagus has not gone down. None of the corporate savings lightened the consumer's load.

The food industry model might well be ready-to-eat breakfast cereals. In that food line, four corporations—Kellogg, General Mills, General Foods and Quaker Oats—control 91 percent of the market. There is no competition on price or quality of the product, nor on the efficiency of the manufacturers. The cereals are essentially the same, with only such artificial differentiations as color or shape. The only "competition" that exists is on merchandising techniques—animated television commercials, radio jingles, package designs, contests and other promotional gimmicks.

Tenneco is trying to become the top dog in the fresh fruit and vegetable market. Its effort, according to a corporate vice president, is to "do what Del Monte has done with canned foods." It is well underway with a marketing scheme for its Sun Giant label. "Establishing brand identification with the consumer is the strategy," wrote a farm reporter approvingly in the *San Francisco Chronicle*. "Produce will be pre-packaged, and each package will bear a smartly prepared advertising booklet pushing the thought that Sun Giant produce is something special."

It gets down to this: packaging and advertising of food are becoming more important pricing factors than the food itself. It is one thing for gasoline or soap to be priced and sold by such artificial gimmicks—but food? Already, food corporations have become the biggest spenders on television advertising.

Higher prices may not be the greatest cost consumers pay for concentration in agriculture. The greatest danger may be the loss of the high-quality food supply that we have had from family farmers. It is a danger posed primarily by three corporate objectives in agriculture: (1) substitution of technology for labor, (2) standardization of the food supply, and (3) introduction of synthetic foods.

For the past thirty years there has been a technological revolution in agriculture, largely financed by taxpayers through the land grant colleges. Genetically-designed melons, pesticides for all occasions, mechanically-harvested strawberries, cattle fattened on drugs, red wax for apples, chemically-skinned catfish and a vast array of other gadgetry are products of the technological fervor that has gripped agriculture since World War II. Although this arsenal has been developed in the name of consumers and family farmers, it was in fact designed for and to the specifications of corporate agribusiness.

Corporate tomatoes today are assembled as though they were bars of soap. Genetically-tailored, these beauties are mechanically-harvested, chemically-ripened, electronically-sorted and mechanically-wrapped in cellophane. Rutgers University recently announced development of a new breed of tomato for this assembly-line process, naming it the "Red Rock." The University of California, finally admitting to consumers that today's manufactured tomatoes have lost taste, announced in 1972 that scientists there have isolated 70 chemicals that cause tomato flavor and that can be artificially injected back into their product. Harvard's Dr. Jean Mayer, former nutrition advisor to President Nixon, was horrified by a Purdue University tomato that was being heralded as the commercial comer because of its particularly red color and uniform shape. "When ripe," Professor Mayer complained, "it will contain at best approximately half the vitamin A content of the varieties of tomatoes presently on the market."

Consumers who wonder what happened to the taste of chickens can be enlightened by Harrison Wellford's description of today's corporate chicken factories:

> The chicken which used to run free to scratch and root in the soil until time for slaughter, now spends its short life in a 12-by-18 inch cage crowded up against three other birds. His day may consist of sixteen hours of artificial light in a totally programmed environment. Crowding favors disease by creating stress and aiding the buildup of harmful bacteria and parasites, such as coddidia. The chicken's feed, therefore, is sprinkled with antibiotic drugs. Other drugs, including arsenic, are fed to increase the rate at which the chicken matures and gains weight. Before going to market, chickens may also be bathed in tetracyclines (antibiotics) or sorbic acid to extend their shelf life. In addition, the bird's chemical diet may contain coloring additives to give their flesh a desired yellow tint.

USDA—initials which used to stand for farmers in the minds of consumers—now conjure up such companion initials as DES, PCB, 2,4,5,-T, DMN and other chemicals and drugs out of the agribusiness medicine chest. The food industry even is having major factory recalls—for example, iceberg lettuce from California went to market in January with Monitor-4 pesticide residues on it and had to be taken back.

Robert Rodale, the editor of *Organic Gardening and Farming*, told a Senate committee last year that agribusiness considers soil to be like the styrofoam material used for arranging flowers. "It is a convenient way to hold up plants and get water to the roots, while the fertilizer companies and pesticide companies and machinery companies do things to the plants—feed it—force feed it and make tremendous profits as a result."

It is the brave new agriculture. Food products are "engineered" to conform with a heavily-advertised image of what they "ought" to look like. Tomatoes are picture-book red, but they are not soft, they have no tomato smell and they lack tomato taste. Pull down a husk of corn in the supermarket and the kernels look big and ripe, but back home those kernels turn out to be filled with water rather than taste.

America's food manufacturers have not been content merely

to tamper with nature's work. They have entered into direct competition with nature by making ersatz "food" in the laboratory. Even the USDA cafeteria has quit offering milk (much less cream) for coffee drinkers; now it's a sterilized, non-dairy "lightener" that is poured into the cup.

Lemon ice box pie without lemons, hamburger without meat, tomato juice without tomatoes and cheese without milk are just a few of the synthetics offered for sale today, many of them under old and trusted brand names. Good Humor has been peddling ice cream in America's neighborhoods for years. Now owned by the English conglomerate Unilever, Good Humor recently began advertising a new ice cream bar named "Whammys". The big selling point of "Whammys" is that they do not drip. How can an ice cream bar not drip? Answer: take the cream out of ice cream and replace it with a heavy dose of chemical emulsifiers.

Fleischmann's, a division of Standard Brands, is known for its margarine. Last spring, in a flurry of national advertising, Fleischmann's moved into competition with chickens. The company is offering a concoction called Egg Beaters—a frozen cholesterol-free egg substitute. "Fleischmann's makes sensible eating delicious," reads the slogan on the package. You might question that claim if you read on down into the small print, where the list of ingredients includes emulsifiers (vegetable lecithin, mono and diglycerides and propylene glycol mono-stearate), cellulose and anthan gums, trisodium and triethyl citrate, aluminum sulfate, artificial coloring and—to meet the claim that it has "all the good taste of farm fresh eggs"—artificial flavor. If that doesn't whet your appetite, neither will the price. A package of Egg Beaters, which claims to be the equivalent of eight large eggs, averages out to 10 cents an egg, while a large, Grade A version of the real thing will cost you only 6 cents each.

What can be done? The only effective barrier to the industrialization of food is consumer action. Family farmers are already in the fight, but they are reduced—by lack of power—to waging a defensive battle. Real power rests with consumers. They must recognize their stake in family agriculture and wage a major food offensive.

Congressional power today is in urban hands. Those voters will determine the direction of agricultural policy. As desperate as it may appear, big city Congressmen represent the last exit off the road to corporate farms and food.

The Family Farm Is the Most Efficient Unit of Production

Even the USDA will sometimes admit that the family-run operation is equally as efficient or more efficient at production than the large corporate farm, and that the advantages of the corporate farm lie in the tax laws, easier access to credit and vertical integration. In 1967, a USDA economist, J. Patrick Madden, reviewed 138 studies on the production costs of different size farms and found mechanized 1- and 2-man farms to be consistently the most efficient. The results of Madden's survey were published by the USDA's Economic Research Service as a technical report, Economies of Size In Farming. *Here, Angus McDonald, former Washington representative for the National Farmers Union, summarizes the Madden report.*

——————————————— Angus McDonald

Over the years there has been a vast propaganda campaign designed to convince the American people that the family farm is inefficient and that super-farms, owned and operated by millionaires and conglomerate corporations, represent the wave of the future.

Swept under the rug, ignored and suppressed are many studies which prove without any reasonable doubt that the small or medium-sized unit is more efficient than the large corporate unit.

These studies, based on solid facts, are not wishful thinking. They are the result of hundreds of analyses of the costs and gross profits of many types of farming, including fruit, grain, livestock, cotton, vegetables, alfalfa and dairy. Here are a few examples:

Fruit Farms in California

On non-mechanical peach farms in the Marysville area of

California, average production cost per ton declined up to a productive unit of about 60 acres. Beyond that size, slight reductions in harvesting costs and machinery investment per acre were realized, but these were offset by higher costs of hired supervision.

On mechanized peach farms the average cost declined up to a farm size of between 90 and 110 acres. After that point there was no reduction in cost on larger units.

Iowa Cash Grain and Crop-Livestock Farms

Hilly farms in southern Iowa showed lowest costs for units of about 320 to 360 acres. This represented a two-man operation and a three-plow tractor. In northeast Iowa, there was little difference in costs between 400- and 800-acre units.

Irrigated Cotton Farms

A study of Texas high plains farms concluded that a one-man farm with adequate capital could be as efficient as any of the larger farms. A one-man farm of 440 acres, with 102 acres of cotton and six-row machinery resulted in an expenditure of 71 cents for every dollar of gross income. None of the larger farms could go below this.

On heavy soil in Fresno County, California, costs of producing cotton proved to be lowest on a four-man farm of 1,134 acres. On light soils a 710, four-man farm proved to be most efficient. A one-man, 193-acre farm had a cost-revenue ratio of 0.83, the four-man farm had a cost-revenue ratio of 0.76. There was no increase in efficiency after this point.

Imperial Valley Vegetable Farms

This particular study concluded that with contract services, long-run costs are constant from the very small farms up to 2,400 acres. Another conclusion was that the Imperial Valley farmer achieves no advantage in owning equipment and actually has advantages over larger farms which own equipment used at less than full capacity. This assumes that contract facilities are available for the small and medium-sized farms. The general conclusion is that there are no significant economies based on size.

Kern County Cash Crop Farms

In this area of California the 640-acre unit was most efficient. After that point costs per revenue dollar began to climb.

Oregon Wheat Farms

One-man wheat farms achieved lower average costs than two- or three-man farms. On farms smaller than 1,000 acres the costs were slightly higher. Increases in size beyond 1,000 acres resulted in increased costs.

Dairy Farms

The most efficient unit in New England was a two-man operation with 70 cows and costs estimated at $2,000 a year for labor and management. However, if no charge is made for labor, the one-man farm with 35 cows achieved lower costs.

In Iowa there was only a slight reduction in costs as herds were expanded from 34 to 58 cows. In Arizona, average costs declined sharply up to a herd of 150-head, but management difficulties typically occurred when the herd reached 150 to 175 cows.

In Minnesota the two-man dairy with 87 cows and 490 acres was just a shade more efficient than the one-man, 48 cow, 290-acre operation.

Feedlots

A USDA study concludes that economies of size are attainable in a size range of 1500 to 5000 head. Beyond this point the cost curve declines slightly, but the savings are insignificant. Other studies indicate that gigantic feedlots are apt to be much less efficient because they are not operated at full capacity. Consequently the percentage of fixed costs are greater than in the small feedlot.

The Land Grant
College Complex

The land grant colleges were created by Congress to be a kind of people's university, reaching out to serve the needs of rural communities. Instead, they became a handmaiden to corporate agribusiness and are in large part responsible for the sad state of rural America today.

In 1972, the Agribusiness Accountability Project organized a task force to investigate the land grant college complex. The task force conducted an exhaustive study which led to the publication of Hard Tomatoes, Hard Times, *a thoroughly documented critique of the land grant college complex that has stimulated much debate and even some small reforms. Here, Jim Hightower and Susan De Marco summarize the basic findings of the task force.*

Jim Hightower and Susan DeMarco————

The land grant college complex consists of three inter-related units: the colleges of agriculture, created in 1862 and 1890 by two separate Morrill Acts; the state agricultural experiment stations, created in 1887 by the Hatch Act; and the Extension Service, created in 1914 by the Smith-Lever Act to disseminate research to the people.

Reaching into all 50 states, the complex is huge, intricate and expensive. The public's total investment in this complex, including assets, comes to several billion dollars in any given year, paying for everything from test tubes to experimental farms, from chalk to carpeting in the dean's office.

There is no doubt that American agriculture is enormously productive and that this is largely the result of mechanical, chemical, genetical and managerial research conducted by the land grant college complex. But the question is whether the achievements outweigh the failures, whether benefits are overwhelmed by costs.

The focus of agricultural research is warped by the land

89

grant community's fascination with technology, integrated food processes and the like. The distorted research priorities are striking:

—1,129 scientific man-years (smy) on improving the biological efficiency of crops, and only 18 smy on improving rural income.

—842 smy on control of insects, diseases and weeds in crops, and 95 smy to insure food products are free from toxic residues from agricultural sources.

—200 smy on ornamentals, turf and trees for natural beauty, and a sad 7 smy on rural housing.

—88 smy on improving management systems for livestock and poultry production, and 45 smy for improving rural institutions.

—68 smy on marketing firms and system efficiency, and 17 smy on causes and remedies of poverty among rural people.

In fiscal year 1969, a total of nearly 6,000 scientific man-years were spent doing research on all projects at all state-agricultural experiment stations. Based on USDA's research classifications, only 289 of those scientific man-years were expended specifically on "people-oriented" research. That is an allocation to rural people of less than five percent of the total research effort.

An analysis of these latter research projects reveals that the commitment to the needs of people in rural America is even less than appears on the surface. In rural housing, the major share of research has been directed not to those who live in them, but to those who profit from the construction and maintenance of houses—architects, builders, lumber companies and service industries.

Other "people-oriented" projects tend to be irrelevant studies of characteristics stemming more from curiosity than a desire to change conditions. At Cornell, for example, a study found that "employed homemakers have less time for house-keeping tasks than non-employed homemakers." Other projects are just as irrelevant:

—Mississippi State University researchers discovered "that families in poverty are not of a single, homogeneous type."

—The University of Nebraska is at work on a study of "factors affecting age at marriage."

—A regional research study unveiled the fact that "the rural population is dichotomous in racial composition" and "pre-retirement family incomes have a direct bearing upon economic expectations for retirement."

—University of Nebraska researchers surveyed football coaches in the state and got 60 percent agreement "that introduction of a federally-sponsored school breakfast program would benefit the nutritional health of teenage athletes."

The primary beneficiaries of land grant research are agribusiness corporations. These companies envision rural America solely as a factory that will produce food, fiber and profits on a corporate assembly line extending from the fields through the supermarket checkout counters. It is through mechanization research that the land grant colleges are approaching this agribusiness ideal.

Mechanization means more than machinery for planting, thinning, weeding and harvesting. It also means improving on nature's design, *i.e.,* breeding new food varieties that are better adapted to mechanical harvesting. Having built machines, the land grant research teams found it necessary to build a tomato that is hard enough to survive the grip of mechanical "fingers"; redesign the grape so that all the fruit has the good sense to ripen at the same time; and restructure the apple tree so that it grows shorter, leaving the apples less distance to fall to their mechanical catchers. Michigan State University, in a proud report on "tailor-made" vegetables, notes that their scientists are at work on broccoli, tomatoes, cauliflower, cucumbers, snapbeans, lima beans, carrots and asparagus.

If it cannot be done by manipulating genes, land grant scientists reach into their chemical cabinet. Louisiana State University has experimented with the chemical Ethrel to cause hot peppers to ripen at the same time for "once-over" mechanical harvesting. Scientists at Michigan State University are using chemicals to reduce the cherry's resistance to the tug of mechanical pickers. And a combination of ferric ammonia citrate and erythorbic acid is being used at Texas A&M to loosen fruit before machine harvesting.

Once harvested, food products must be sorted for size and ripeness. Again, land grant college engineers have produced a mechanical answer. North Carolina State University, for example, has designed and developed an automatic machine "which dynamically examines blueberries according to maturity." The University of California and other colleges have scientists at work on machinery that will sort tomatoes.

Who is helped and who is hurt by this research?

It is the largest-scale growers, the farm machinery and chemicals input companies and the processors who are the primary beneficiaries. Machinery companies such as John Deere, International Harvester, Massey-Ferguson, Allis-Chalmer and J.I. Case almost continually engage in cooperative research efforts at land grant colleges. These corporations contribute money and some of their own research personnel to help land grant scientists develop machinery. In return, they are able to incorporate technological advances in their own products. In some cases they actually receive exclusive licenses to manufacture and sell the products of tax-paid research.

If mechanization research has been a boon to agribusiness, it has been a bane to millions of rural Americans. Farmworkers have been the earliest victims. There were 4.3 million hired farmworkers in 1950. Twenty years later that number had fallen to 3.5 million. As a group, those laborers averaged $1,083 for doing farm work in 1970, making them among the very poorest of America's employed poor.

Farmworkers have not been compensated for jobs lost to mechanization research. They were not consulted when that research was designed, and their needs were not a part of the research that resulted. They simply were left to fend on their own—no re-training, no effort to find new jobs for them, no unemployment compensation, no research to help them adjust to the changes that came out of the land grant colleges.

Independent family farmers also have been largely ignored by the land grant colleges. Mechanization research by land grant colleges is either irrelevant or only incidentally adaptable to the needs of some 87 to 99 percent of America's farmers. The public subsidy for mechanization actually has weakened the competitive position of the family farmer. Taxpayers, through the land grant college complex, have given corporate producers a technological arsenal specifically suited to their scale of operation and designed to increase their efficiency and profits. The independent family farmer is left to strain his private resources to the breaking point in a desperate effort to clamber aboard the technological treadmill.

Like the farmworker, the average farmer is not invited into the land grant laboratories to design research. If he were, the research package would include machines useful on smaller acreages, assistance to cooperative ownership systems, and a heavy emphasis on new credit schemes. In short, there would be a deliberate effort to extend mechanization benefits to all, with an emphasis on at least maintaining the competitive position of the family farm in relation to agribusiness corporations. These efforts do not exist, or exist only in a token way.

Mechanization also has a serious impact on the consumer. Land grant researchers are not eager to confront the question of food quality, choosing instead to dwell on the benefits that food engineering offers agribusiness. The University of Florida, for example, recently developed a new fresh market tomato (the MH-1) for machine harvesting. In describing the characteristics that make this tomato so desirable for machine harvest, the University pointed to "the thick walls, firm flesh, and freedom from cracks." It may be a little tough for the consumer, but agricultural research can't please everyone. The MH-1, which will eliminate the jobs of thousands of Florida farm workers who now hand-pick tomatoes for the fresh market, is designed to be harvested green and to be "ripened" in storage by application of ethylene gas.

Convenience to the processor often outweighs taste for the consumer. For example, University of Wisconsin researchers developed a process for making mozarella cheese in five and a half minutes, compared to the usual time of four hours. The flavor of the final product is reported to be "mild, but satisfactory for the normal uses."

The colleges also are engaged in "selling" the consumer on products he neither wants nor needs, and they are using tax money for food research and development that should be privately financed. At Virginia Polytechnic Institute, for example, eight separate studies have been conducted to determine if people would buy apple and grapefruit juice blended. Other projects involve surveys to determine what influences the shopper's decision-making. If this research is useful to anyone, it is food marketers and advertisers, and reports on this research make clear that those firms are the primary recipients of the results. The corporations who benefit from this research should pay for it and conduct it themselves.

The consumer is not just studied and "sold" by land grant research; he is also fooled. Chickens have been fed the plant compound Xanthophyll to give their skin "a pleasing yellow tinge," and several projects have been undertaken to develop spray-on coatings to enhance the appearance of apples, peaches, citrus and tomatoes. Other cosmetic research projects that are underway at land grant colleges include:

—Iowa State University is conducting packaging studies which indicate that color stays bright longer when bacon is vacuum-packed or sealed in a package containing carbon dioxide in place of air, thus contributing to "more consumer appeal."

—Scientists at South Carolina's agricultural experiment station have shown that fluorescent light treatment can increase the red color in machine-picked tomatoes and cause their texture and taste to be "similar to vine-ripened tomatoes."

—Kansas State University Extension Service, noting that apples sell on the basis of appearance rather than nutrition, urged growers to have a beautiful product. To make the produce more appealing, mirrors and lights in supermarket produce cases were cited as effective selling techniques.

Service to agribusiness is not by coincidence. In dozens of ways, corporate agribusiness gets into the land-grant complex. It is welcomed there by administrators, academics, scientists and researchers who share the agribusinessman's vision of integrated, automated agriculture.

Corporate executives sit on college boards of trustees, purchase research from experiment stations, hire land-grant academics as private consultants, advise and are advised by land grant officials, go to Washington and state capitols to urge more public money for land-grant research, publish and distribute the writings of academics, provide scholarships and other educational support, invite land-grant participation in their industrial conferences and sponsor foundations that extend both grants and recognition to the land grant community.

Money is the web of the tight relationship between agribusiness and the land-grant complex. It is not that a huge sum of money is given—industry gave $12 million directly to state experiment stations for research in 1969. Rather it is that enough money is given to influence research done with public funds.

At least 23 land-grant colleges have established private, tax-exempt foundations to handle grants and contracts coming into their institutions for research. Through these curious mechanisms, corporations funnel money to public universities to conduct research. By this shell game, private research can be undertaken without obligation to report publicly the names of the corporations that are making research grants, the amounts of those grants, the purpose of those grants or the terms under which the grants are made.

These foundations also handle patents for the colleges. When a corporation invests in research through a foundation, it is done normally with the understanding that the corporation will have first shot at a license on any patented process or product that results. On research patents that do not result from corporate grants, the procedure for licensing is just as cozy. At

Purdue University, for example, a list is drawn of responsible companies that might have an interest in the process or product, and the corporations are approached one by one until there is a taker.

There is nothing inevitable about agribusiness domination of agriculture. Had the land-grant community chosen to put its time, money, expertise, and technology into rural people, rather than into corporate pockets, rural America today might have been a place where millions could live and work in dignity. It is time to re-orient the colleges so that they begin to act in the public interest.

Organic Technology

Most tax-funded agricultural research in the United States has focused on machines and chemicals that benefit large-scale farmers, while small farmers and especially organic farmers have been written off as obsolete or downright "kooky." Here, Robert Rodale argues that this emphasis can be and should be turned around.

Rodale is the editor of Organic Gardening and Farming *magazine. These remarks are taken from his statement to the Senate Migratory Labor Subcommittee.*

Robert Rodale

Researchers at the land-grant colleges have continually used advancing technology to replace human hands with machines, chemicals and special varieties of crops. The result has been more food produced by each farmer and on each acre, but at the same time much displacement of people to the cities, high costs for welfare, other social disruption and often sad environmental consequences.

Organic gardeners and farmers are the remnants of the many millions of people who at one time constituted the yeoman core of American stability and strength. We are largely the little people still living on the land, not the businessmen farmers. We grow vegetables and fruits on small plots, using natural and non-chemical methods because we have found by experience that those methods are very effective. We concentrate on building the fertility of the soil because we know that a fertile soil produces abundant crops with much less work and expense than a depleted soil.

The amount of help that land-grant colleges have given to organically-oriented people over the years is hardly enough to be worth mentioning. Some techniques of conventional agriculture are used on organic gardens and farms. Improved tractors and tillers are a help, and so are new biological controls for insects. But the great bulk of new chemicals and machines and ideas coming out of the land-grant colleges have been anti-organic in their orientation, and of no use to us.

The real tragedy is that the agriculture colleges have often attacked the organic people—who really are the only farmers and gardeners completely in tune with the environment—simply to create a smokescreen to mask the stupidity of their technological policies. We are the kooks and the nuts, they say, while the chemical-spraying farmer, sitting on his mammoth tractor, is supposedly nature's nobleman. The real truth, which these land-grant college scientists don't want to face, is that if organic systems were used universally in agriculture and in urban life, our country would be much better fed and stronger in many ways.

The land-grant colleges should use their scientific resources to create a new generation of what I call the soft technology of farming. They should create machines and techniques that are better and smaller at the same time, instead of concentrating on large-scale techniques that always end up replacing people. We organic people do not want to go back to the old ways. We are not advocating a return to primitive farming, where people are worn out by hard work by the time they are 40. We want a new, ecologically-oriented agriculture that can be made possible by the intelligent application of the best scientific thinking to our problems.

Here are some of the areas in which scientific effort is needed.

Energy. Conventional farm technology is based on the use of *stored* solar energy in the form of processed coal, oil, gas and soluble fertilizer deposits. By contrast, all farming prior to 100 years ago, and organic farming today, operated primarily on *current* solar energy falling on crop lands.

Absorption and conversion of current solar energy is far from complete using present methods. Through photosynthesis, plants convert only a small fraction of the sun's energy into usable food. By extending the growing season through natural means, ways can be found to increase the conversion rate of solar energy on small farms. More intensive methods for growing fruits and vegetables also make much more efficient use of the sun's energy than does the growing of crops such as wheat, corn and soybeans.

With new technology based on more scientific input, solar energy can also be used on small farms for home heating, waste conversion and increased movement of water from the subsoil to the surface by way of deep-rooting plants. Other sources of energy can also be tapped for small-farm use. Wind-power generation can be perfected, and organic wastes can be used to produce methane gas for heating, lighting and even for powering of automobiles. Power storage systems suited for small-farm use can also be developed.

Waste conversion and fertilizer production. Ways can be developed to make many waste products of urban living into valuable fertilizers, with less labor and handling than is currently needed. Present technology is adequate to convert almost any organic waste to a fertilizer or soil conditioner, but process-costs need to be reduced. Also, urban governments seeking to dispose of wastes should be directed to small organic farms.

Machinery. Agricultural engineering departments of land-grant colleges should cease work on machines for large farmers and work only on machines that will make small farmers more practical and competitive. The rotary tiller is such a machine. Using small power units, it enables large-scale gardeners to do a thorough job of tilling the soil. It is essentially a miniaturization of the traditional plow-harrow machines.

Similar miniaturizations of all farm machines are needed. Some are already available, particularly tractors and related equipment. But work is needed to develop miniaturized harvesting equipment that will enable individual farm workers to compete with large-scale machines.

Biological insect control. Much good work has already been done toward finding natural substitutes for toxic chemical pesticides, thanks to both the ecology movement and the realization some years back that pesticides are too expensive and have a limited useful life because of the build-up of insect resistance.

Increased scientific efforts in the biological control area are necessary. Of great interest are recent discoveries indicating that plants, animals and insects (and perhaps even man) are tied together in a chemical communication network. The active agents of this network are pheremones, essentially airborne or waterborne hormones. Pheremones provide the answer to many questions that have puzzled both biologists and farmers, and point toward new culture methods that eliminate toxic risks and lower costs of production. However, chemical pesticides cover up or interfere with the pheremone network, so the system of natural food production is not always compatible with partial use of chemicals, as in integrated control.

Education. City and farm people should be taught to appreciate the virtues of small-scale production. Present education practices are directed toward creating agricultural specialists, or people motivated toward working in agribusiness operations.

Marketing. Here is an area of great potential benefit for the small-farm movement. Intensive scientific and business efforts should be directed toward perfecting methods of getting fresh, relatively unprocessed food quickly and cheaply from farm to consumer. Cooperatives can be of help. So can improved packaging and shipping techniques.

A continuation of present land-grant college actions and philosophy will insure that there is no alternative to the destructive course of U.S. agriculture. Farms will get fewer and fewer, and farming profits will go to bigger and bigger conglomerates. More and more people who want to remain on the land will find their own tax dollars used to fight against the very agricultural alternative they are trying to create.

Existing efforts of land-grant colleges are clearly not enough. Land-grant college advisory committees and policies must aggressively develop solutions to the problems plaguing family farmers and rural communities. Half-hearted efforts—as we have seen in the past—get us nowhere. We need people in official capacities in the USDA and land-grant college to say: "I am ready and able to support specific research and programs which will help more people make a better living on the farm....I am ready and able to support specific alternatives to our present agricultural system."

This does not mean a condemnation of everything now going on in the agricultural system. All I am saying is that those who seek change should have official recognition and a substantial amount of the dollars now being expended, and that people in high places should not be so quick to condemn those who would alter the agricultural *status quo*.

The dirt farmer is gone, the agricultural engineer has taken over.

John Vachon, FSA. *Harrowing and planting corn; Iowa, 1940.*

Fred S. Witte, USDA. *Four-wheel drive diesel tractor; Texas, 1972.*

Technology has made the farmer an industrialist

Fred S. Witte, USDA. *Cultivating cotton; Texas, 1972.*

Marion Post-Wolcott, FSA. *Picking cotton; Mississippi, 1939.*

Arthur Rothstein, FSA. *Farmer and potato digger; Colorado, 1939.*

© George Ballis. *Sorting potatoes; California.*

...and the farmworker a factory-worker.

Bob Griffith. *Tomato picking machine; New Jersey, 1973.*

T. L. Gettings. *Pennsylvania, 1974.*

T. L. Gettings. *Vegetable stand; Pennsylvania, 1974.*

The alternatives are disappearing.

Bob Griffith. *Pennsylvania, 1974.*

USDA. *Melon processing plant; California, 1958.*

USDA. *Packing grapes; California, 1965.*

T. L. Gettings. *Pennsylvania, 1973.*

Part IV
Water and Energy

The Battle
for Acreage Limitation

The distribution of land in the United States has been closely tied to the distribution of water rights, especially in the arid West where land is of little value unless it is irrigated. Water, of course, is as much a public resource as is land itself, and when the public spends money on massive projects to irrigate dry land or protect flood-prone land, it has a right to determine how the benefits of those expenditures shall be distributed.

Paul S. Taylor has been vigorously involved in the fight for fair distribution of water rights since the 1930s, and has been an inspiration to a whole generation of land reformers. He is now professor emeritus of economics at the University of California, Berkeley. The following article was presented at the First National Conference on Land Reform.

Paul S. Taylor

The fight over water in the West is as old as the dream to "make the desert blossom as the rose" through irrigation. At the center of the struggle is the limitation on the water that any one individual may receive—the amount of water needed to irrigate 160 acres.

In 1902, on the floor of the House, the chairman of the committee in charge of the first reclamation bill gave assurance to Congress that

> in order that no such lands may be held in large quantities or by non-resident owners, it is provided that no water right for more than 160 acres shall be sold to any landowner, who must also be a resident or occupant of his land. This provision was drawn with a view to breaking up any large land holdings...in the vicinity of government works and to insure occupancy by the owner of the land reclaimed.

During a floor debate a New York Congressman, skeptical that these assurances could be relied upon, warned that behind this scheme, egging it on, encouraging it, (are) the great railroad interests of the West, who own millions of acres of these arid lands, now useless, and the very moment that we, at the public expense, establish or construct these irrigation works and reservoirs, you will find multiplied by 10, and in some instances by 20, the value of now worthless land.

The skeptical New Yorker turned out to have a point. Three years after Congress enacted the 160-acre limit and the residency requirement, the now-familiar attacks upon the law began. The first effort of the big Western land owners was to try to persuade the 1905 session of the citizens' National Irrigation Congress that acreage limitation was a mistake. Their plea was rejected emphatically. A few years later, however, they successfully obtained a ruling from the Interior Department that effectively voided the requirement of residency. Only in 1973 was the residency requirement revived by a federal district court decision in San Diego.

When the Salt River Project in Arizona was built, the Interior Department supplied the water but made no move to enforce the 160-acre law. Similarly, in the closing days of the Hoover Administration, the Interior Department simply ruled the law inapplicable to California's Imperial Valley, although it is served by the Boulder Canyon Reclamation Project.

In the early years of the New Deal a new tactic appeared, designed to remove acreage limitation through Congressional action, project by project. The Colorado-Big Thompson project was so exempted, with no committee hearings, no floor debate, no record vote, and with Interior Department comment on the bill furnished by an official acting in the absence from Washington of Secretary Harold L. Ickes. Similar tactics produced exemptions for the Salt River Project in Arizona and the Nevada-Truckee Project in Nevada.

The same technique was attempted in 1944 to exempt the giant Central Valley project in California from acreage limitation. No mention was made of exemption during protracted hearings on a rivers and harbors bill. Thus the proposal to exempt came to the floor as a committee amendment without warning, and the House passed the exemption within minutes.

With the issue out in the open, it became a different story. Public hearings were held, first in Washington and then in California. As a result of the hearings the Senate removed the exemption from the bill. Nevertheless the exemption was restored to the bill in conference. Replete with appropriations for local rivers and harbors construction projects, the fate of the entire "pork barrel" was tied to the 160-acre exemption. Notwithstanding its obvious attractiveness to members of Congress throughout the country, the bill went down to defeat when Senator Robert M. LaFollette, Jr. of Wisconsin threatened to deliver a three-hour speech against exemption if the bill were pressed.

A fresh attempt to persuade Congress to remove the acreage limitation and residency requirement from the statute books was made in the Republican 80th Congress in 1947. All six Senators from California, Colorado and Texas joined to seek exemption for projects within their states. Among the witnesses against the exemption were spokesmen from organized labor, the Grange, Farmers Union, National Catholic Rural Life Conference, American Legion, American Veterans Committee and Veterans of Foreign Wars. Testimony filled 1,300 pages and the bill died in committee.

In the meantime, pressure from large landowners succeeded in 1944 in blocking construction of a dam on the Kings River in California by the Bureau of Reclamation and, instead, giving authorization to the Army Engineers. Initially the Army Engineers were not governed by the acreage limitation and residency law. As the authorization bill ran its course through Congress, however, the Roosevelt Administration insisted that it be amended and the Senator in charge assured one and all before FDR affixed his signature to the bill that the wishes of the Administration had been complied with. Nevertheless, 28 years later, in 1972, a federal district court held the 160-acre law inapplicable to lands in the irrigation district receiving water from the dam on the Kings River.

The tactic of seeking piecemeal erosion of the acreage limit yielded results in other project areas. President Truman vetoed exemption of the San Luis Valley Project in Colorado the first time it passed. In 1952, however, a modified version became law, raising the limitation to 480 acres and stating that the change furnished no general precedent. In 1954 Congress exempted the Owl Creek, Wyoming, and Santa Maria, California, projects. In each instance reasons special to the particular project were cited as justification.

The next try was to remove the limitation on all projects financed with less than $5 million of federal money, i.e., on all "small" reclamation projects. The "Engle formula" included in the small reclamation projects bill gave owners of excess lands an opportunity to buy their way out of compliance with the acreage limitation law by making a modest money payment. This was struck out by the Senate but restored in conference and whisked through the Senate during the rush to adjourn. No explanation was offered for failure to honor the customary request by Senator Paul Douglas, who had led the successful fight to kill the excess land owners' option, that he be notified when the bill returned to the Senate after conference with the option restored. One is reminded of the observation by William Ewart Gladstone that "Property is vigilant, active, sleepless; if ever it seems to slumber, be sure that one eye is open."

The next drive against acreage limitation was couched as a flank attack. While the unsuccessful 1944 effort to exempt California's Central Valley project was still in progress, an alternative was being readied in case it should fail. Since California state law, although approving acreage limitation on federal projects within the state, was silent as to state-owned projects, the plan was to sidestep the 160-acre limitation by having the state of California take over the Central Valley project, paying the entire bill.

The first obstacle facing this plan was that it would be very costly. In addition, Secretary Ickes stated that federal acreage limitation would follow the transfer of title. So the tactic was modified: the state would construct a separate project to transfer northern water southward. One obstacle remained. Since geography offered only one route for moving water southward, whether federal or state, the state needed permission to share federal facilities—reservoir, canal and pumps—without obligation to observe the federal acreage limitation. Spokesmen for California's large landowners requested exemption for the state project from the 160-acre limit. Congress debated the request for four days in the Senate and two in the House. Both houses approved the joint use of facilities, but rejected the exemption from federal law. Nevertheless, when the contract covering the transaction appeared under the auspices of Secretary of Interior Stewart L. Udall and Governor Edmund G. Brown, obligation to observe the acreage limit was omitted. Now, with the state water project almost completed, four small farmers have taken the acreage limit issue to federal court.

The stakes in the battle for acreage limitation in the West are tremendous. Of the 25.3 million acres which have been reclaimed through irrigation in 17 states, federal projects account for 6.5 million acres. This was done at a total construction cost of $10 billion, with $2 billion of that spent since 1958, primarily in the Colorado Basin and California's Central Valley.

It is important to note that water subsidies from federal irrigation projects are estimated to range from $600 to $2,000 an acre. It is well also not to overlook the fact that reclamation, despite its location in the West, gives away public waters and public moneys that belong to the entire nation.

The unceasing attack upon this 70-year-old national policy is only one side of the history of reclamation law. On the other side are the efforts to preserve and make the 160-acre limit effective. Fighting on this side have been organized labor, church social action, family farm, veterans' and environmental groups. Since the 1950s, a few family farmers and landless persons—and even the U.S. Attorney General in some cases—have brought several lawsuits seeking to promote enforcement of the law. Lower court decisions have gone both ways, and are on appeal.

In 1972 seven Congressmen and four Senators sponsored a bill to create a Reclamation Lands Authority empowered to purchase excess lands at the pre-water price stipulated by present law. The aims are to promote a better distribution of land and to recapture windfall profits for the public treasury. The Authority could hold open a door of opportunity for the landless. It could check urban sprawl over prime agricultural land, preserve green-belts and open spaces. The practical question of the moment is: Will Congress respond?

Mississippi Levees and the Big Plantations

Like irrigation projects in the West, flood control projects in the South and Midwest have transformed relatively useless land into higher productive farms. No acreage limitation or residency requirement accompanied the expenditure of public funds for flood control, however. One consequence, as Paul Wallace Gates points out, was the subsidization of huge plantations in the Mississippi delta. The following selection is excerpted from Gates' testimony before the Senate Migratory Labor Subcommittee.

―Paul Wallace Gates

One of the numerous government programs that has drastically changed land values and encouraged concentration of ownership has been the construction of giant levees on the banks of Middle Western and Southern rivers to keep out the flood waters of the spring run-off. The levees have made possible the transformation of low-lying and perennially flooded areas of little value into the richest cotton, rice and cane-producing land in the South, and with little or no cost to the owners.

It is in the levee-protected region of the delta of Mississippi that one of the largest foreign ownerships of agricultural land—38,000 acres—is to be found. The four principal states benefiting from this levee construction had, in 1959, 2,581 farms of more than 2,000 acres and 109 of more than 10,000 acres.

FARMS IN EXCESS OF 2,000 ACRES				
Farms of over 2,000 acres		Farms of over 10,000 acres		
State	Number	Acres	Number	Acres
Alabama	733	2,955,763	30	520,206
Arkansas	526	1,911,108	17	249,652
Louisiana	562	2,550,611	39	724,682
Mississippi	760	2,847,077	23	421,800

Such concentration of ownership was made possible by the lavish way the federal government gave away what seemed to be comparatively worthless swampland to the states which, in turn, conveyed it to land companies, speculators and influential politicians on the understanding that they would drain the land, which they failed to do. Finally, the government was persuaded to build the levees and to provide a great boon to the landowners whose holdings acquired high value. No attempt was made to assess abutting property owners for the bonus they received.

Pumping the Ogallala Reservoir

In many parts of the country, non-renewable underground water supplies are being pumped dry by large corporate farms and energy companies. Here, Victor K. Ray reports on the "mining" of the Ogallala Reservoir under eastern Colorado.

Ray is assistant to the president of the National Farmers Union. This report is taken from his 1968 booklet, The Corporate Invasion of American Agriculture.

Victor K. Ray

Underlying a 9,000-square mile region of eastern Colorado is the Ogallala Reservoir. Within the past decade, large corporations have begun pumping water from this formation, using huge self-propelled irrigation systems that pivot at the center of each quarter-section, throwing out torrents of water into the fields.

Amer Lehman, a farmer at Idalia, felt so strongly about the pumping that he went to Omaha to tell the Monopoly Subcommittee of the Senate Small Business Committee that "this resource can be exhausted in a generation or less in some areas."

Recharge of this reservoir, Lehman reported, is only by rainfall and is balanced by outflow.

He said: "Consequently, any withdrawal from the reservoir is in effect 'mining' of the water. Thus the critical policy question in the development of the non-renewable resource revolves around how rapidly it will be exhausted and who will benefit from its use."

This is not the first time the resources of the Great Plains have been exploited, Lehman said. The first time came in the 1870s when men from London, Boston, Paris and New York formed syndicates to run cattle on the open range. Overgrazing, homesteaders and the great cattle-killing blizzard of the winter of 1885-86 brought that era to an end. It was not until World War I that the next period of exploitation occurred. It was a time of great need for food. The first big tractors came to turn the sod. The drought of the 1930s—and the wind—wrote the epitaph of that boom in the dust.

The next period of destruction came with the drought of the 1950s. The government soil bank came to the rescue and many fields were returned to grass again. Now the corporate irrigation pumps are lowering the water table perceptibly every year, and it is a permanent lowering. The Colorado State University Experiment Station at Fort Collins pointed out that replenishment is only about half an inch a year, and that one well pumping 500 gallons per minute would withdraw the equivalent of one-half inch of water from under a section of land in less than two weeks. Many corporate farmers are withdrawing at the rate of 1,000 gallons a minute from under each quarter section of land!

If the water of the Ogallala is depleted, as it now seems bound to be, the area will return to dust—this time for good. It has all of the makings of the "American Sahara."

The late William Vogt in "Road to Survival" developed an equation—a bio-equation, he called it—that would be instructive and timely for the residents of the land above the Ogallala. Vogt, a recognized authority on conservation and land usage, was chief of conservation for the Pan American Union. He expressed the bio-equation $C=B:E$. C stands for "carrying capacity," the ability of a region to provide food, drink and shelter to the creatures that live in it. B means "biotic potential," the ability of the land to produce plants for shelter, clothing and food. E stands for "environmental resistance," or the limitations that any environment, including the part of it contrived and complicated by man, places on the biotic potential or productive ability.

"The carrying capacity is the resultant of the ratio between the other two factors," said Vogt.

He said: "We cannot force land into the pattern we wish to impose upon it, but must fit the use to the land, its capabilities and its limitations. All management of the land should be designed to maintain as favorable a ratio as possible on the right-hand side of the formula ($C=B:E$), improving it where possible, and at the very least maintaining the status quo. Where the relationship is deteriorating we must inevitably reduce the demand on the carrying capacity—either by a lower living standard or by a reduced population."

There is yet time to save the Great Plains. The patterns of ownership and, thus, the patterns of destruction of the physical resources, are still diverse. Perhaps...perhaps there is still time.

Hidden Dimensions
of the Energy Crisis

One crucial but little-noticed aspect of the energy crisis is the enormous demand that new energy development will place on the nation's water supply. This "water crunch" will be particularly acute in the West, where most of the energy development will take place and where water is scarce to begin with. One result, according to Michael Perelman and Hugh Gardner, will be less water for agriculture and higher food prices.

Perelman is a professor of agricultural economics at California State University, Chico. Gardner is a free-lance writer in San Francisco who specializes in land-related issues. The following article originally appeared in People & Land, *the newspaper of the land reform movement.*

——— *Michael Perelman and Hugh Gardner*

Now that the oil bubble has burst, the race is on to develop substitute processes to satisfy our seemingly endless demands for energy. Corporate executives and federal officials have focused primarily on three such substitutes: nuclear fission, coal burning and gasification, and oil shale.

There are many nasty problems with each of these techniques, but one they all have in common—and perhaps the worst of all in the long run—is that they all require enormous amounts of water. So much water, in fact, that an unintended consequence of solving the energy crisis may be the creation of a far more serious food and water crisis.

Consider, for instance, the nuclear reactor that the Los Angeles Department of Water and Power is considering locating in the San Joaquin Valley. Besides an unspecified quantity of agricultural drainage water, the plant is expected to take about 100,000 acre-feet of water each year from the California Aqueduct. Translated, that works out to the consumption of at least 33 billion gallons of water a year, or about 4 billion flushes of the average toilet.

Strip mining the West for coal will create even more dramatic water demands. A recent report by the National Academy of Sciences warns that strip mining and processing of Western coal will raise "staggering" water problems that have not yet been addressed. Western strip mining, says the report, may disrupt water supplies to the point where "the direct and indirect consequences may be far more important than the ability to reclaim the actual site of the mining."

Regardless of whether the coal is burned to produce electricity or converted to gas, either process will use vast amounts of water, a precious resource in the arid West. But despite the fact that private coal operators are going ahead full speed with *their* plans, the N.A.S. report states that "there is little evidence that adequate mechanisms for planning exist at any governmental level."

The dimension of this conflict between coal and water becomes apparent with a little multiplication. There are now 176 potential sites for coal gasification, each requiring about 25,000 acre-feet of water per year to operate. One acre-foot of water equals 325,851 gallons, so what it all adds up to is the prospect of the consumption of almost 1½ trillion gallons a year. To put this figure in more understandable terms, coal gasification may require roughly three times as much water as the total annual flow of the California Water Project, one of the world's largest.

Already the Intake Water Company, a subsidiary of Tenneco, has filed an appropriation request for over 80,000 acre-feet of water from the Yellowstone River in Montana, which is approximately one-fourth of the total flow of that river. The U.S. Bureau of Reclamation has granted Tenneco a license to build a pump plant on the Yellowstone despite the fact that an environmental impact study has not been completed—an apparent violation of the law.

The water demands of oil shale mining may be still more severe, so much so that a recent AEC study indicates that shale oil cannot become a major U.S. energy source. The Department of Interior's impact statement for the prototype oil shale leasing program estimates that a mature 1 million barrel per day shale industry will require from 121,000 to 189,000 acre-feet of water annually. Bear in mind that there are at least 1 trillion barrels of shale oil buried in Colorado, enough for about 2,740 years of mining at this rate. The actual "mature shale industry" will likely be a great deal larger than Interior suggests, especially with the recent quantum leap in posted prices for oil.

The effects of such drastic reductions in irrigation water will inevitably be a decline in Western agriculture. The cost of these projects for the American consumer, first in terms of water and then in terms of food, may be enormous.

In California, for instance, sophisticated linear programming techniques indicate that agricultural water use is insensitive to price until it reaches a cost of about $18 per acre-foot, which is 80 percent above current undervalued water prices. At this point, water usage falls off drastically. If, for example, irrigation in California should be reduced by 50 percent, the result would be a $1.5 billion reduction in crop production. And when these crops disappear from the market, prices on what's left would rise to the tune of $2 billion.

Thus the consumer gets hit from two sides at once. Energy will cost more because water costs more, and food will cost more for the same reason, in addition to being more scarce.

Moreover, the withdrawal of cheap supplies of irrigation water comes at a time when U.S. agriculture should be coming to grips with the rapid depletion in its stocks of fossil water as well as fossil fuel. At present the U.S. is using twice as much water from groundwater reserves as is being naturally recharged into these reserves.

In short, the United States must quickly turn its attention to solar, geothermal, wind and other sources of energy that are not only non-polluting, but also not dependent on vast supplies of water. Otherwise, the rush to coal, shale and fission will leave us gasping for water in the future.

We might get by with less flushing, but can we stop eating too?

Energy
and the Public Lands

Today's energy crisis is closely related to public land policies established many years ago. This is because the federal government has given away valuable energy resources to a few monopolistic companies. Here, Peter Barnes discusses some alternatives to the continued giveaway of public energy resources. This article first appeared in People & Land.

Peter Barnes

America does have an energy crisis, but it is a crisis of control, not supply.

There are plenty of energy resources in the United States. Some, like coal, oil and natural gas, have been widely exploited. Others, like the sun, the wind, the tides and the heat of the earth, are just beginning to be tapped.

The trouble is that energy sources in America are controlled by a small cartel of corporations whose goal is maximum private profit. Supplies and prices are manipulated so as to minimize competition. New energy sources such as solar and geothermal power are not developed because they would diminish the profits from existing energy systems.

The major oil companies control enormous amounts of land in the United States and offshore. (See Table.) Most of these energy-rich acres were obtained in one way or another from the public domain.

Still, the striking fact is that most of our remaining energy reserves are on or under public land. Over half of our oil and natural gas reserves, 40 percent of our coal and uranium, 80 percent of our oil shale and 60 percent of our geothermal resources lie under public lands. They are owned, in other words, by the people.

The critical question over the next few years is what will be

125

done with the energy resources that the people own. Will they be given away to the same profit-seeking cartel that created the present "crisis"? Or will they be developed on a non-profit basis in the public interest?

Unfortunately, the track record of the federal government is not good. While other countries have been moving more and more toward public ownership of energy resources, the United States remains a firm believer in giving to the few what belongs to us all.

The standard practice of the Interior Department is to lease energy resources on public lands to private bidders. In areas where the resources are known to be substantial, bidding is usually competitive, elsewhere it is first-come, first-served, or based on random drawings. Generally the bidder pays an initial bonus plus a 12½ percent royalty when production begins.

The recent "crisis" has spurred the Interior Department to accelerate its leasing of public resources to private corporations. Thus, within the past year, hundreds of thousands of acres of off-shore oil and gas reserves, oil shale lands in Colorado and geothermal sites in California have been turned over to oil companies. This is in addition to the hundreds of thousands of acres of western coal rights that were leased to the same corporations in the years prior to 1973.

If the federal government wants to spur competition within the energy industry, the last thing it should do is to give control of new energy resources to the same corporations that control the present ones. A study by the Federal Power Commission found that eight major corporations already lease 74 percent of the available oil and gas reserves on federal lands.

Other studies have pointed out that the corporations that control oil production and refining have now moved into competing sources of energy: 20 of the largest oil companies account for 60 percent of American natural gas production and reserves, 29 of the top 50 coal companies are subsidiaries of oil companies, and oil companies own nearly 45 percent of known domestic uranium reserves. This kind of monopoly control of energy needs to be broken, not strengthened, but it won't be broken unless present leasing policies are changed.

Consider what is happening to the people's geothermal resources. Potential geothermal sites abound throughout the western states, and the National Science Foundation estimates that geothermal power could supply as much as a fifth of the nation's electricity by 1985.

Naturally, oil companies such as Shell, Phillips, Union, Getty, Sun, Standard of California and Occidental Petroleum are trying to get control of geothermal energy. If they succeed, the cost to consumers could come to millions, if not billions of dollars.

Union Oil, for example, claims rights to underground steam in the Geysers area north of San Francisco, the only site in the United States at which geothermal power is not being generated commercially. In fact, there is some dispute over whether Union Oil actually owns the geothermal rights it claims. The Justice Department has contended in a lawsuit, now on appeal, that geothermal rights are among the mineral rights that were reserved to the United States when western land was homesteaded a century ago.

In any case, assuming possession, Union Oil signed an exclusive contract to sell steam to Pacific Gas and Electric, a private utility that has recently applied for massive increases in electrical rates charged to consumers. When a group of non-profit municipal companies tried to purchase steam from Union, the oil company refused to sell. Significantly, the Union-PG&E contract calls for the price of steam to be pegged to the price of other competing fuels.

There are alternatives to the continued giveaway of public energy resources. For example, geothermal energy in the West could be developed by the Bureau of Reclamation, like hydro-power was, with preference in the sale of electricity going to municipal and consumer-owned utilities. Similarly, coal in Appalachia and the Plains states could be developed by locally-owned public utility districts. A bill to this effect was recently introduced in the Wyoming legislature with support from rural electric co-ops.

The most comprehensive alternative yet proposed is a bill introduced by Senator Adlai E. Stevenson III of Illinois to establish a Federal Oil and Gas Corporation, patterned after TVA. Co-sponsoring the bill are Senators Abourezk, Hart, Kennedy, McGovern, McIntyre, Metcalf, Mondale and Moss.

The Federal Oil and Gas Corporation would have access to publicly-owned oil and gas rights, as well as the power to acquire energy rights on private lands. It could enter into the full range of activity necessary for the exploration, development, refining, transportation and marketing of petroleum and gas products.

Such a corporation would accomplish three things, according to Stevenson. "First, the corporation would develop publicly owned oil and gas resources in order to satisfy national energy needs rather than to maximize private sector profits. Second, it would stimulate competition in the petroleum business. Third, it would provide the public with knowledge of the actual cost of producing oil and gas so that public policy can be geared to the nation's interest."

Stevenson noted numerous foreign examples of public oil corporations—BP in Britain, CFP in France, ENI in Italy, Petrobas in Brazil, Pemex in Mexico, YPF in Argentina, Oil India and many others. Only America, it seems, encourages private monopoly profits at the expense of people's needs and rights.

ENERGY COMPANY LAND.*

Company	U.S. Acreage
Standard of Indiana	20.3 million
Texaco	9.9 million
Mobil	7.8 million
Gulf	7.5 million
Phillips Petroleum	5.3 million
Standard of Calif.	5.2 million
Continental	4.5 million
Union	4.1 million

Source: Moody's Industrial Manual.

*Includes acreage owned and leased, some of which is off-shore Acreages for companies such as Shell, Exxon and ARCO were not available.

Bureau of Reclamation, National Archives. *Construction of the Arrowrock dam; Idaho, 191*.

Family in the sixth year of their wait for irrigation water, Ute Mountains, 1913.

Irrigation under a North Platte River project, 1909.

The first water projects captured precious water
in huge dams and distributed it to
homesteaders for irrigation.

Bureau of Reclamation, National Archives. *Irrigated orchards, truck gardens and hay   fields; Colorado, 1910.*

Fred S. Witte, USDA. *Sprinkler irrigation system; Texas, 1972.*

Harry R. Steele, USDA. *Four-thousand-gallon-per-minute irrigation well; Colorado, 1967.*

Bob Fitch. *Worker and irrigation ditches; California.*

But new irrigation techniques are squandering
water, at a time when it is in greater demand,
from more quarters, than ever before.

Edwin W. Cole, USDA. *Irrigated farmland; Nebraska, 1967.*

Bob Griffith. *Nuclear power plant; New Jersey, 1974.*

Part V
Taxes

Sowing the Till

Tax policies have an enormous impact on the economic and social structure of rural America. Generally speaking, both federal and local tax laws favor large absentee-owned investors at the expense of working people and small farmers. Loopholes in the federal income tax code make it attractive for corporations and wealthy city dwellers to become farm owners for tax purposes. At the same time, the local property tax tends to underassess large landholdings.

In the following article, Jeanne Dangerfield examines tax-loss farming and its impact on real farmers. The paper was originally published by the Agribusiness Accountability Project. Dangerfield is now a graduate student in public policy at the University of California, Berkeley. A. V. Krebs assisted on the research for this paper.

Jeanne Dangerfield

While many farmers have been losing money and going under, an increasing number of corporations and wealthy urbanites have learned how to lose at farming and still get away with a profit. Rather than working the land, they work the tax laws.

In detail, it's complicated. In concept, it's simple: Lose money in farming and write those losses off against non-farm income. The impact is to lower the amount of income that is taxable. There's a bonus: The losses are not real, only paper losses. That is because the costs of "farming" can be written off in one year, even though the product will not be sold until another year. Thus, there are tax losses this year, profits next year. And those profits can be re-invested for still another tax loss. In 1972, these farm losses cost the U.S. Treasury over $840 million.

The key to tax shelter farming is a series of tax loopholes built into revenue acts that go back to 1916. The first was in the Revenue Act of 1916. It gave farmers the option of using either the "cash accounting method" used by individuals on their tax returns, or the "accrual accounting method", required of all other

139

businesses. Under the accrual method, an expense or sale is ruled to be effective at the time the goods purchased actually change hands. Under the cash accounting method, an expense or sale is considered incurred at the moment the money changes hands.

If a cash farmer pays for $1,000 worth of food in December, he can deduct the cost in that year, even if the feed is not delivered until January of the following year. Under the accrual method, the farmer could not take the deduction until the feed is actually delivered.

Cash accounting is important to both the farmer and the farm investor. To the farmer, cash accounting means some flexibility in adjusting year-to-year income; it also simplifies bookkeeping chores.

To the tax-loss investor, who is generally able to afford accountants and bookkeepers, cash accounting creates artificial losses by allowing premature deductions of expenses against high non-farm income. This lets him postpone paying taxes on that percentage of his income equivalent to the amount of his farm deductions. In effect, he gets an interest-free loan from the government. When the product is finally sold and profit realized, the public's interest-free "loan" to the investor can be extended if the investor chooses to reinvest his profits in another farm venture.

The actual subsidy received by the tax-loss investor increases in proportion to his tax bracket. For example, an investor in the 50 percent tax bracket would normally pay half of every $1,000 of income in taxes. If he can deduct a $1,000 feed expense from his tax bill, however, he has, in effect paid only $500 for $1,000 worth of feed.

Another loophole involves deductions on capital assets— i.e., assets that are not incorporated in any one final product, but that can be used to develop many end products over a period of time. In non-farm businesses, the cost of these assets is generally recovered through depreciation, which involves deducting a certain percentage of the cost of the asset over a number of years equal to its useful life.

Orchards, vineyards and dairy and breeding herds, because they are not actually products to be sold, but rather produce commodities that are sold, are capital assets. The cost of maintenance, upkeep and development of these capital assets is called a capital expenditure and in non-farm businesses would not be immediately deductible. Under the Revenue Acts of 1916 and 1919, however, farmers and farm investors receive a special privilege: the costs of raising livestock held for draft, breeding or dairy purposes, and the costs involved in developing vineyards and fruit and nut orchards, are all fully deductible, even though they are capital expenditures.

The Revenue Act of 1942 included another special provision for farmers and farm investors: capital gains treatment on the sale of assets such as trees and vines. A later court decision further expanded this provision to include draft and dairy breeding animals. This means that income from sales of these capital assets, which have been held for a specific minimum period of time, are taxed at rates equivalent to half the person's regular tax bracket.

As with other special tax provisions for agriculture, this loophole works out better for wealthy investors than for real farmers. First, the benefits increase proportionately to the taxpayer's income bracket. And since, in many cases a real farmer would have to sell his source of support in order to take advantage of the capital gains opportunity, this tax "benefit" puts teeth in the old adage that farmers live poor and die rich.

Cash accounting, deduction of capital expenditures and capital gains treatment are the keys to tax shelter farming, but there are certain other benefits available to farmers which have implications for farm investors. Under the Revenue Act of 1971, the investment credit was made available for purchase of livestock and various kinds of real property, such as feed bins and farm buildings. The investment credit allows a dollar-for-dollar reduction of the tax bill of an amount equal to 7 percent of the cost of eligible property. Another inducement to investing in ranching is the availability of accelerated depreciation rule (ADR) on certain assets, including cattle and real property.

For individuals, the primary mechanism which makes "farmers" out of tax shelter investors is the limited partnership. This is an organizational form that has been used in oil, gas and real estate for some time, but is relatively new in agricultural enterprises. A limited partnership allows the pass-through of profits and losses—and tax deferrals—straight to the individual partners. The partnership itself is not taxed, but rather each partner is taxed in proportion to his share of the venture.

Feedlots and food distributors, such as Montana Beef Industries and Cal-Maine Foods, often set up partnerships to obtain clients and capital for their services. Railroads, oil companies and utilities figure prominently in the organization of limited partnerships, since they have land available for such projects. Insurance companies, too, are appearing as farm venture backers, partly because they hold the mortgages on a large amount of farm land. Southern Pacific, Atlantic Richfield, Buttes Gas and Oil, Kaiser Aetna, Apache Corporation and

Hartford Life Insurance are just a few of the companies involved in farming through this method.

Another possibility for the investor would be to enter into a contract with an agency that specialized in managing farm investments. Oppenheimer Industries is one firm that will purchase breeder or feeder cattle for clients, contract with ranchers or feedlots to care for them, and arrange putting the cattle on the market. Kaiser Aetna's Ventura Operations in California will manage the absentee owner's citrus or walnut groves.

A third possibility for the tax-loss investor is to make direct contact with his investment by personally arranging to buy land or cattle, for example. In order to take advantage of tax benefits, the investor must be considered to be engaged in farming for a profit. If the IRS determines the investor-farmer is just in it for pleasure, recreation or some other non-business purpose, his deductions may be disallowed.

A principle common to most farm investments is the concept of leveraging—that is, using one's actual cash in the venture as collateral for a loan to increase the total available working capital. Tax laws provide that an investor can deduct not only the expenses incurred by the actual cost to him of his investment, but also expenses incurred by borrowed money. In other words, if the investor's actual cash contribution is $5,000, and that money is used as collateral to borrow an additional $10,000, the investor may be able to make deductions worth two to three times the real cost of his investment.

Not all areas of agriculture are equally attractive to the tax-loss farmer. The areas which currently seem most attractive are orchard and vineyard development, cattle breeding herds and cattle feeding programs. Within the areas having the best potential for the tax-loss farmer, certain commodities tend to come in and out of popularity. In the 1960s investor money was going into citrus and almonds. But the Tax Reform Act of 1969 required the costs of developing citrus and almonds to be capitalized, rather than keeping these costs deductible, so investors turned to pistachios, apricots and walnuts. Now because of rising popularity and increased consumption of wine in the U.S., investors are rushing into grapes.

For the full-time farmer trying to make a living from his crops, tax-loss farmers pose a serious problem. At recent Senate hearings on Land Ownership, Use and Distribution in California, one family farmer described the impact of an oil company's quickie tax dodge. The company planted several thousand acres of cling peaches on the western side of the Central Valley. As a result, the market was glutted and many growers were forced to let their peaches rot on the trees. The oil company was left with a tax write-off and the farmers were left with all the peaches they could eat.

Confucius said that "the best fertilizer is the footsteps of the landowner." The current tax system works against that wisdom by fostering absentee ownership. As one agri-deal ad puts it, "The prime market for the new agribusiness participations are those legions of desk-bound executives who have always thought they wanted to get closer to the land if only through proxy."

Property Tax Evasion

Throughout the country, large landholdings are notoriously underassessed. This is particularly true of the holdings of coal, timber and oil companies. A minimal remedy would be taxation of all kinds and sizes of property at the same rate. Even better would be a progressive property tax that, like the income tax, taxed larger units at a higher rate than smaller units.

In the following selection, consumer advocate Ralph Nader discusses some of the most blatant property tax abuses. His statement is taken from testimony before the Senate Select Committee on Equal Educational Opportunity, September 30, 1971.

— *Ralph Nader*

The underassessment of coal begins with self-assessment. Local assessors have no idea who owns what and how much it is worth. The owners of coal lands simply tell their version of what they own, where, and its value. Ill-equipped, frequently untrained local assessors have no way to check the owner's statement. The "Tax Commissioner" of Knott County, Kentucky, described the process thus to the *St. Louis Post-Dispatch:*

> The coal companies pretty much set their own assessments....
> We have no system for finding out what they own. Like they
> may tell us they own 50 acres at a certain place, when
> actually they own 500 acres....If a company says an area is
> barren or mined out, we have to accept it.

Or as one local Tax Commissioner told the *Appalachia Lookout*, "People (meaning coal companies) just paid what they thought they should. Still do, mostly."

This system is not exactly air-tight. In fact, a good deal of rich coal property—one authority puts the figure at tens of thousands of acres—never gets onto the tax rolls at all. A fact-finding team appointed by the Pike County, Kentucky school board in 1967 found that 40 to 60 percent of the county's land was either unlisted or underassessed. That year the Pike County schools had a deficit of almost $113,000 and 45 percent of the people were below the poverty level. Yet at the same time $65 million worth of coal was being hauled out of the county.

Even when Kentucky coal land does get onto the tax rolls, the owners, some of the largest and most profitable corporations in the nation, pay hardly a pittance. "Thousands of acres of coal land worth $200 to $300 an acre get on the assessment books at $2 an acre," the *Louisville Courier-Journal* said in 1965. For example, National Steel Company currently is developing a huge new mining complex on 14,200 acres of coal land in Knott County. It is building a large, ultra-modern tipple and a preparation plant that is expected to produce 1,250,000 tons of first-quality coal annually. A new railroad is being built to get at this coal. The owner of this tract of coal land, Elkhorn Coal Corporation, has paid its shareholders a staggering 35 percent of its gross receipts in dividends. Yet Elkhorn Coal Corporation has been paying Knott County taxes of less than 22 cents per acre on land so rich as to warrant the new railroad and preparation plant.

Or consider Harlan County, where U.S. Steel has strip-mined the Big Black Mountain, the tallest in the state, into a colossal wreck. In 1966 more than $30 million worth of coal was mined out of Harlan County, and U.S. Steel's subsidiary, U.S. Coal and Coke, was the county's largest single producer. U.S. Steel paid taxes of only $34,500 to the county on two producing mines valued—probably by itself—at $9,300,000. In Arizona, U.S. Steel would have paid almost ten times as much on the same operation. With that much extra revenue from U.S. Steel, Harlan County could have provided close to twice the $41 per pupil it could afford in 1968—still not much, but at least a start.

In Kentucky, property taxes levied are not always property taxes paid. Several years ago a reporter from the Hazard, Kentucky, *Herald* found that large mining companies owed Perry County over $75,000 in back taxes. The New York Mining Company alone owed over $4,200. Apparently the county was making no effort to collect.

Throughout Appalachia, the story is the same. The people are poor, the schools are poor, but the owners of coal land enjoy a property tax field day. Tennessee's five most prolific coal counties, which produced 6 million tons of coal in 1970, are losing several thousand dollars per year in property tax revenues, according to a study done at Vanderbilt University last summer. Coal land owners control over one-third of the total land area of the five counties but they provide less than four percent of the property tax revenues. One owner collects royalties of $4,500 per week on land assessed at $20-25 an acre—the same value the county assigns to unused woodland and one-quarter of what it assesses farms!

The pattern continues across the country. The largest and wealthiest corporations flout or evade the property tax laws, victimizing the public schools. A report released recently by a team of law students led by Maine lawyer Richard Spencer disclosed that Maine has been losing over $1 million annually in property tax revenues because its timberlands are underassessed. According to the report, the State Property Tax Division does not even have a trained forester to check the work of the private appraisal firm, James W. Sewall, Inc., that assesses the timber land under contract. The president of that appraisal company, which also performs substantial private work for the timber companies, is Joseph Sewall, chairman of the appropriations committee in the Maine state legislature.

In Augusta, Georgia, a so-called Committee of 100 of "prominent citizens" touched off an epidemic of underassessments some ten years ago by offering illegal tax concessions to firms as an inducement to locate there. The concessions were supposed to be temporary and available only to new industries; but nobody enforced these restrictions and in time the prominent 100 had filched, according to the Richmond County Property Owner's Association, $300 million worth of property from the assessment rolls. Meanwhile many of the county's schools are on double sessions and there is a shortage of 147 classrooms, not including 119 "nonstandard" ones.

School districts in Texas have fared little better. In the Permian Basin the underassessment of oil and gas properties belonging to some of the world's largest producers has cost one school district at least $1 million a year for the last seven years. A 1970 study of oil and gas properties by Texas University law students in Ector County, Texas, found that producing properties were undervalued by about 56 percent and that a non-producing property which Texaco had leased for $460,500 was not on the assessment rolls at all. Homes, on the other hand, were assessed at very close to actual market value.

A survey of timber land in six counties and four school districts in east Texas by the same law students disclosed a pattern of underassessment which, if projected over the entire 37-county east Texas region, signified a loss of approximately $38 million in local revenues each year. In the Newton Independent School District alone, six companies, including Champion-U.S. Plywood and the Kirby Corporation, underpaid by more than $133,000 in 1969.

The states themselves have been at least silent partners in much of the systematic undertaxation, the magnitude of which has barely been suggested. Weak local property tax administration, and a lack of effective checks and appeals procedures for the small taxpayer, isolate abuses from public scrutiny and pressure and lets them flourish. Weak property tax administration, and an absence of procedures through which citizens can protect their interests, do not just happen. A state legislature must establish and then preside over them. Property tax administration in many states is a shambles because, in a manner of speaking, the state legislatures have wanted it that way.

The states are vying to offer "favorable tax climates" that will hold old industry and lure new industry in. But a "tax climate" which suits business is not always the one which can provide the public services, including education, that people need. What the businesses won't pay falls upon the individual taxpayer.

Special
Farmland Assessment

To discourage farmers from selling their land to suburban subdividers, many states have granted special property tax relief to open space landowners. Generally, these laws require a contract between the county and the landowner: if the landowner agrees not to develop his property for a given period of years, the county will assess the property at its value as farmland, rather than at its higher potential value as a housing subdivision.

The success of these laws has varied from state to state; the California law, known as the Williamson Act, has been a notable failure. Here, in 1973 testimony before the Assembly Select Committee on Open Space Lands, Peter Barnes analyzes the California experience.

———Peter Barnes

The California Land Conservation Act, more commonly known as the Williamson Act, is a classic example of money misspent for a worthy objective.

The stated objective of the Williamson Act is to preserve open space and prime agricultural land. The mechanism employed is use-value rather than market-value assessment. The theory is that rising property taxes brought about by encroaching suburbia force farmers to sell prematurely to developers. If farmers are relieved of the tax burden created by the rising market value of their land, the argument runs, they'll continue to farm and development will be checked.

It's a nice theory, but it hasn't worked in practice. The Act gives too much to the wrong people for no reason. Most of the land it reduces taxes on is not threatened with development; the owners of this land receive a public subsidy without returning a public benefit. Where land *is* threatened with development—e.g., along the coast, in the Santa Clara Valley or in the Santa Monica Mountains—the Act has provided neither sufficient incentives nor sufficient penalties to deter that development.

To whom and for what does the act confer public subsidies? The major beneficiaries, according to the Legislative Analyst, are not farmers but "the owners of range and watershed lands, whose lands have little prospect of coming under heavy urban pressure or being used for agricultural purpose." According to a survey undertaken by former state Senator George Danielson, 87 percent of the lands benefiting from the Williamson Act are not prime agricultural lands, and only 6 percent are within three miles of cities.

The biggest recipients of Williamson Act tax breaks are the big corporate landowners of rural California. According to Ronald Welch of the State Board of Equalization, more than 25 percent of the land covered by Williamson Act contracts is owned by 12 large corporations. Together they enjoyed reduced property tax assessments totalling more than $44 million in 1972.

These giant beneficiaries cannot by the farthest stretch of the imagination be described as farmers pressed by rising property taxes. Many of them are in the *Fortune* list of America's 500 largest corporations. Most receive a wide variety of other public subsidies in the form of income tax preferences, crop payments and low-cost irrigation water. One publishes the state's major daily newspaper. It is a joke to think that the Williamson Act encourages these beneficiaries not to develop land that can be profitably developed; if anything, it encourages them, and others like them, to acquire land for long-term speculative gain.

The burden of these pointless subsidies to large landowners falls largely upon those least able to pay—nearby residents who are landless. A study by Doug Kaplan, a summer intern with the Center for Rural Studies, found that residents of Hanford, the seat of Kings County, have seen their general county tax rate jump 73 percent in two years, in large part because two-thirds of the land in the county is under Williamson Act contract. Soaring residential property taxes are passed on to renters, many of whom are unemployed or low-income farmworkers. The situation is much the same, although perhaps not so extreme, in other rural counties.

State reimbursement of some of the revenues lost by counties under the Williamson Act reduces, but does not eliminate, the shifting of the property tax burden from large landowners to landless farmworkers and small homeowners. The total tax shift, local and statewide, was approximately $40 million in 1971. It has surely risen considerably since then.

Is the Williamson Act worth saving? Only if it is radically amended, and only if we cease pretending that it is a means to preserve open space. The chief amendment I would propose would be to restrict the application of use-value assessment to actual resident farmers. To define an "actual resident farmer" is not a simple matter, but I would suggest these guidelines: (1) that the farmer live on, or within 25 miles of, the land receiving the tax reduction; (2) that he shall not have received more than $20,000 in non-farm income during any of the past three years; (3) and that his acreage eligible for use-value assessment be limited to 160 acres of irrigated land and 640 acres of non-irrigated land.

Adoption of this kind of amendment would at least have the effect of taking the rich off welfare: it would exclude from Williamson Act benefits the large conglomerates and tax-loss syndicates that are already too prominent in rural California. Whether it would have the effect of preserving open space, or keeping family farmers in business, is more doubtful, since many factors other than rising property taxes are involved in the decision of farmers to sell or develop their land. Commodity price levels, affecting the farmer's rate of return on both his equity and his labor, are a primary factor. So is the undeniable lure of reaping socially-created gains in land value. As Jonathan Rowe of the Tax Reform Research Group has pointed out, farmers— unlike white collar and factory workers—do not receive pensions or retirement benefits. What they have for retirement is the capital gain in their land value—a "pension" that can only be collected by selling.

If the Williamson Act—even a radically amended version— is no way to preserve open space, what is? One approach is zoning and land use regulation, as embodied, for example, in the recent coastal protection initiative. Given the persistence and political clout of developers, however, I am skeptical that zoning enforced by regulatory commissions is an effective long-range means to preserve open space.

Another approach might be to tax those who develop, rather than reduce taxes on those who don't. This was the approach recommended by the recent Nader Task Force on California Land. The report urged the state, using its police powers, to freeze-zone the land according to its present use. Then, anyone wishing to develop land further would have to pay a substantial "zoning-up" tax. This approach would have the merit of taxing the relatively wealthy rather than the relatively poor, but I'm not sure it would preserve open space. More probably the "zoning-up" tax would be absorbed as another cost of development, and passed on to those who buy or rent structures in the newly developed area.

The only sure way to preserve open space is for the public to buy it—either through outright purchase or the purchase of development rights. The appropriate way to finance public land acquisition is to tax those who profit from socially-created rises in land value. I would recommend, however, that public land acquisition not be limited to scenic and recreation areas for the well-to-do. Funds should also be allocated to low-income groups for the acquisition of land for housing and new family farms.

In sum: the Williamson Act is a costly, inequitable and wholly ineffective way of preserving open space, and ought to be discarded as a means to that end. Instead of bestowing tax relief upon un-needy large landowners, the state should tax those who profit from socially-created land increments and use the revenues thus raised (which could be substantial) to purchase land for open space *and* for housing and farms for low-income families.

The Severance Tax

Tax laws, if properly written, can be a potent instrument of reform. One tax that would be particularly beneficial to resource-rich rural areas is the severance tax, which is a tax on the extraction of minerals, timber and other depletable resources. Texas, Louisiana, Oklahoma and Alaska raise considerable revenue through a severance tax on oil, but most coal producing states lose millions of dollars by not imposing a similar tax. Here, Paul J. Kaufman, an attorney and former West Virginia state senator, tells what a severance tax would mean for Appalachia. This statement was presented at the First National Conference on Land Reform.

Paul J. Kaufman

At least $502 billion worth of coal, oil, gas and timber has been removed from Appalachia during the past 130 years. Had these riches been taxed at a rate of five cents per dollar, the tax take (counting all sources) for the coal-bearing Appalachian states would have doubled over the past century. Putting it another way, all state taxes paid by Appalachians during the past century amounted to less than would have been produced by a five percent severance tax. The benefits in terms of roads, schools, health care, housing and other badly needed public services would have been enormous.

In West Virginia, in the year 1970 alone, just under $50 million could have been raised by a five percent severance tax for the use of poverty-bound mountaineers. But West Virginia has never had a severance tax. Kentucky finally enacted a modest tax on minerals about a year ago. Its contitutionality immediately came under attack by the coal industry which for so long prevented its enactment. One former Governor of West Virginia during his administration had the effrontery to urge the passage of a tax on coal. He was literally chased from the state, became an alcoholic and wound up as a Chicago taxi-cab driver.

Most of Appalachia, or at least most of the mineral wealth of Appalachia, is owned by non-Appalachian multi-national corpor-

152

ations. Not only are the inhabitants denied the use and benefit of "their" land, but the exploitation and abuses to which both land and people have been subjected over the years by absentee interests are beyond measure.

One way to enable the people to protect and enjoy the land on which they live is to expropriate it for them as has been done in Central American countries previously colonized by huge American corporations. This is not likely to happen.

Local acquisition of the land through public utility districts, cooperative development, land trusts and the like also has possibilities. But adequate depletion taxes, as opposed to depletion allowances as we have come to know them, can be utilized in short order to enable the people to share, in a small way, the great wealth being held just beyond their reach.

It has been suggested that state legislatures should be encouraged to take all revenues from severance taxes and place them in trust for use at some future date to purchase coal-bearing lands and make these lands part of the public domain. It is ironic that not even minerals underlying national and state preserves in Appalachia today are owned by the public. In many instances they are owned by private industry which has the right to destroy the surface whenever necessary to extract what lies beneath.

A severance tax may be levied as a percentage of gross sales or on a per unit basis, such as so much per ton in the case of coal, so much per barrel in the case of oil, and so much per thousand cubic feet in the case of gas. U.S. Senator Lee Metcalf and others have advocated a federal severance tax with provisions for full credits to companies that pay a little tax in the states in which they do business. Such a federal severance tax has the obvious advantage of prompting enactment of state severance taxes by eliminating any competitive disadvantage which might otherwise befall an enterprising state government.

Heretofore, a federal severance tax has been opposed by the United Mine Workers of America as well as the National Coal Association. However, the new leadership of U.M.W. sees things differently and the prospects for Congressional action on this subject are brighter than before.

Taxes
for Land Acquisition

The ideal way to use taxes as an instrument of reform is to link them directly to desired objectives—for example, land redistribution. In the following selection, John McClaughry outlines several imaginative ways to tie land-related taxes to land reform. The statement was presented to the First National Conference on Land Reform.

McClaughry, a Republican, is a former Vermont legislator and White House aide who currently directs the Institute for Liberty and Community in Concord, Vermont.

— *John McClaughry*

Various intricate tax provisions may be used to encourage donors to convey lands to a land trust program, but in general, any program for acquiring and conveying land, or holding it in trust for specified uses, requires some source of financing.

Perhaps the most logical and possibly most lucrative source of revenue to finance a land reform program is the *increment value tax*, sometimes called the "unearned increment tax" or "capital gains tax". This tax is based on the theory that much of the increase in value of undeveloped land is due to society, and not to the efforts of the land's owner.

This is arguably true in two senses. Where there is a public investment—a highway, airport, sewer line—adjacent land increases in value because of it. Even where there is no specifically identifiable public investment, the changing preferences of consumers, such as urban residents seeking a country home, may drive up the price for land. Since the increment is "unearned" by the land owner, "society" has a right to claim the value of the increment through taxation.

The classic argument for the site value tax, advocated by Henry George in his *Progress and Poverty* (1879), is equally applicable to the land increment value tax. The difference is that

George's argument applied to the total value of the land; the increment value tax applies only to the rise in value experienced during the time the land has been held by the current owner, and is imposed only at the time of transfer.

There are several important considerations to be understood in connection with increment value taxation. First, allowance must always be made for the value of actual improvements made by the landowner, such as drainage, clearing, access roads, etc., which create "earned" increments of value.

Second, there is the troublesome question of the "value" of risk accepted by the owner of undeveloped land. When a speculator purchases a parcel of land, he satisfies the needs of the previous owner who wishes to exchange illiquid land for a liquid asset, money. The speculator converts his liquid assets and credit to an illiquid asset, land. He holds the land hoping to become a seller later on at a profit. This is not an inconsiderable service. In some cases the speculator may take a beating, as when a glue factory or junkyard locates near his parcel. How to set a price on this "earned" service of the speculator in creating liquidity for a seller and absorbing risk has never been satisfactorily dealt with. Much of the oratory condemning land speculation fails to recognize that the speculator does perform a service for which he is entitled, in fairness, to some reward.

Third, it should be noted that increment values are customarily taxed annually in every property tax system. This is because land that has increased in value will be reappraised (sooner or later) to the higher value, increasing the amount of taxes payable annually on it. The increment value tax in effect double taxes this increment, by imposing a second tax on it at the time of transfer.

Finally, there is a question of fairness involved in moving from a system based on landowners right to increment value to a system based on the right of society to that value. Whether or not the present system is deemed proper and just, it exists, and many present system is deemed proper and just, it exists, and many people have acted in the reasonable expectation that it will continue. If a wholly new system, such as the public right to enjoy "unearned increment," is to be substituted, in fairness those who have acted on the basis of the previous system should, at least in the early years of the new system, receive some allowance from the public.

These considerations are not offered to discredit the idea of an increment value tax on land, but merely to suggest that the practical implementation of such a tax contains some serious difficulties that deserve to be addressed.

Mabel Walker of the Tax Institute of America reports in the

August, 1971 *Tax Policy* that a land increment value tax has been tried in Austria (1822), imperial China (1890), imperial Germany (1911), Denmark and Taiwan, with varying results, but has rarely been the subject of even serious study in the United States. In 1973, however, the state of Vermont became the first jurisdiction in the country to enact an increment value tax on land. The Vermont law imposes a tax based on both the amount of gain and the length of time the land was held by the seller. The tax does not cover buildings or improvements, and also exempts up to five acres necessary for a dwelling if the dwelling is the principal residence of the seller. The tax is paid by the seller at the time of sale. The basis (tax cost) of the land is that determined under the federal Internal Revenue Code.

Two examples will help make this clear. Suppose a speculator bought a 100-acre parcel of unimproved country land in 1974 for $20,000. Without making any improvements in the land, he sells it in 1977 for $40,000. Having held the land for three years and having sold it for a gain ($20,000) equal to 100 percent of the basis, he would be taxed at 22.5 percent of the gain, or $4,500.

A second example: A speculator buys a 100-acre parcel in 1974 with a residence upon it for $40,000. In 1979 he sells the entire property for $90,000. If half the original basis is allocated to the residence and five acres, then the amount of gain on the remaining 95 acres would be $25,000, or 120 percent of basis. The tax would be, for 120 percent gain and five years ownership, 7.5 percent or $1,875.

These are somewhat overly simplified examples, as they ignore certain exemptions, commissions and sales expenses, and many complications of determining the original basis under IRS rules, but they give a general idea of how the tax is calculated. The tax goes to zero if the property has been held for six years or more.

The purpose of this increment value tax in Vermont was to raise money to fund a property tax relief program totally unrelated to land reform. Governor Salmon promised that under this program no Vermonter would have to pay more than five percent of his income on property taxes on his house and its surrounding acre of land. The Governor also offered considerable oratory to the effect that the increment value tax would stamp out the serpent of land speculation.

As was pointed out by his critics, the Governor can not have it both ways. If the tax is successful in stamping out the serpent of land speculation, there will be no revenue for tax relief. If there is to be tax relief money, land sales must not be taxed out of existence. This is a dilemma that must be faced whenever revenue and social impact are said to be offered in one package.

In practice, the increment value tax considerably dampened sales of land. In fiscal year 1973, for instance, the one-half of one percent Vermont property transfer tax yielded $2,027,000. In the first ten months of fiscal 1974, despite generally higher prices for land, this tax yielded only $1,358,000. If one assumes that transfer of property exempt from the increment value tax continued at their recent trend, the reduction in sales of land subject to the increment value tax must have been extremely pronounced to have produced such a shortfall.

It is most unfortunate that the proceeds of the increment value tax, originating from land transfers, has been tapped for the non-land-related purpose of general property tax relief. It would have been far preferable to use these revenues to fund a Vermont Land Trust, a measure introduced by the writer in the 1972 General Assembly.

As it is, the continual clamor for general tax relief will probably prevent any future diversion of the increment value tax revenues into a land reform or environmental preservation program. This suggests that advocates of land reform in other states should make a strong effort to relate an increment value tax to land reform programs, before competing interests seize upon those revenues to fund their special programs.

A second source of financing for land acquisition is what in Great Britain is known as the *betterment levy*. This tax, in force in Britain from 1967 to 1971, was applied to the increment in value due solely to a change in zoning status. It bore no relation to the length of time the land was held prior to the change, and was subject to a host of adjustments.

Here is, again, an overly simplified example: A hundred acre parcel of open land has been zoned "agricultural conservation". Its value, based on what it should bring on the market for agricultural conservation uses only, is $50 per acre, or $5,000. The owner sees an opportunity to make a profit by converting this parcel to garden apartments, providing he can obtain a change in zoning to "low density residential." He appeals to the planning board for the zoning change, arguing the need for additional garden apartments in the area and the suitability of his parcel for this use. The board agrees and rezones the land "low density residential." For this use, the value of the land now becomes $500 per acre, or $50,000. Leaving aside the numerous adjustments, the owner would be subject to a 40 percent tax on the $45,000 "betterment", or $18,000.

It should be noted that the betterment levy was a not too important part of an extremely strong program of state zoning in Great Britain. According to Professor C. Lowell Harriss, the levy strongly discouraged any increase in land use intensity, and its revenues were small in relation to the administrative costs involved. Its repeal, says Harriss, does not support a rejection of land increment value tax proposals for the United States, especially since repeal came after the adoption of an overlapping capital gains tax in Great Britain.*

It should be noted, too, that when originally conceived in the 1940s in Great Britain, the betterment levy was seen as a source of revenues to compensate landowners whose land values had been reduced by restrictive zoning. That is, when the planning boards increased the value of certain lands by permitting intensive development, and denied the same opportunity to other landowners, the lucky landowners should be taxed to compensate the unlucky ones. This is a complicated subject, but there does seem to be some merit to the argument.

To summarize, the betterment levy might produce some revenues for a land reform program, provided the tax rate is not so high tht it only discourages development; that the administrative complexities are held to a minimum; and that the revenues are not automatically allocated to a compensation fund for landowners whose development rights have been limited by zoning regulations.

A third possible source of tax revenues for land reform is the *property transfer tax*, in effect in Vermont since 1963. The Vermont tax, estimated to produce about $1.9 million in 1974, is levied on the sale price of all real estate at a rate of one half of one percent. Originally this tax was levied to provide funds for tax mapping of the state, but the proceeds were soon diverted into the general fund and the tax mapping was never seriously undertaken. This is unfortunate, because any serious effort at land reform requires a precise tax mapping to ascertain who owns land, where it is, and what it is worth.

The law requires each seller to file a property transfer tax form at the time of transfer, indicating the sale price and other pertinent data. This form is invaluable in helping the state tax department determine tax equalization factors among the various towns, required by Vermont's school aid formula, which is based on real estate wealth per pupil in each town. There have been no administrative complications with this tax.

One unfortunate effect of the property transfer tax has been its disproportionate burden on lower income families. The tax is absorbed in the sale price, which means the poor man must pay the same rate on a modest home as a rich man pays on a chateau. This could be remedied by exempting the first $10,000 from the tax, and making the tax one percent on everything over $10,000, or otherwise graduating the tax.

These possibilities for raising revenues for a land reform program vary in efficacy and must of course be considered within the particular tax structure of each state. Obviously, adoption of one may preclude adoption of one or more of the others, so careful thought must be given as to the most advantageous method.

[1] Harriss, C. Lowell, "Land Value Increment Taxation: Demise of the British Betterment Levy," 25 *National Tax Journal* 567 (December, 1972).

USDA. *Appalachian school and pupils; Kentucky, 1965.*

USDA. *The school water supply; West Virginia, 1962.*

Taxes not collected contribute nothing to schools
or other social institutions,

Russell Lee, FSA. *Sharecropper mother teaches her children; Louisiana, 1939.*

Jack Delano, FSA. *Coal cars; Ohio, 1943.*

William H. Hylton. *Abandoned coal breaker; Pennsylvania, 1968*

...while tax inequities encourage the pillage
of natural resources,

...the growth of agribusiness,
the spread of suburbia.

USDA. *Grape harvesting machinery; Michigan, 1973.*

Bob Griffith. *Orchard; Pennsylvania, 1972.*

T. L. Gettings. *Suburbanization; Pennsylvania, 1972.*

T. L. Gettings. *Pennsylvania, 1973.*

Part VI
Small Towns and Rural Poverty

A Tale of Two Towns

Walter Goldschmidt is a noted anthropologist who launched his career thirty years ago with a landmark study of two small towns in California, Arvin and Dinuba. Goldschmidt was employed at the time by the Bureau of Agricultural Economics of the USDA, and his objective was to learn whether the size of farms made a difference in the life of rural towns and rural people. Then as now, this was a highly controversial subject, and Goldschmidt discovered that his findings were too "hot" for the USDA, which refused to publish them. But the Senate Subcommittee on Small Business did print Goldschmidt's report, and eventually it was published as a book, As You Sow.

In 1972, after devoting most of his academic career to African anthropology, Goldschmidt appeared before Senator Fred Harris' hearing on land monopoly in California to reminisce about his Arvin-Dinuba study. His earlier conclusion was unchanged—indeed, it was strengthened—by the passage of time: small farms make for a better rural society than do large farms.

The following statement is taken from Goldschmidt's testimony at the Harris hearings. He is now a professor at the University of California, Los Angeles.

Walter Goldschmidt ———————————————

It is difficult to prove causation in history, for each society is unique and the forces are complex, but there are few who doubt that the nature of rural land tenure is intimately related to the character of the social order. By and large, where democratic conditions prevail, the man who tilled the soil was a free-holder and in control of his enterprise. Where, on the other hand, farming lands are owned and controlled in urban centers and the men engaged in production are merely peasants, serfs or hired laborers, democratic institutions do not prevail.

Those who framed our Constitution and set the course of American history believed that this relationship was paramount. It lay behind Jeffersonian democracy; it lay behind the

171

Homestead Act, and it lay behind the extension of homestead principles in the development of irrigation under the Reclamation Act.

It is a remarkable fact that in this scientific era, so little empirical research has been done on this vital relationship. Indeed, I know of none other than the one I conducted in 1944, which was published by the U.S. Senate in 1946.[1] This study on the California towns of Arvin and Dinuba was one of "controlled comparison." We selected two towns which, as nearly as was possible, were alike in basic economic factors except that they differed in farm size. In scientific terms we treated farm size as the "independent variable," and examined the character of social life and organization in the two communities as the "dependent variable."

We found that the two towns varied remarkably—variances that were consistent, statistically significant, and all in support of the principle that independent family farms create a healthier rural community. Though the total dollar volume of agricultural production was the same, the communities differed in the following important ways:

—The small farm community had more institutions for democratic decision making and a much broader participation in such activities by its citizenry.

—The small farms supported about 20 percent more people and at a measurably higher level of living.

—The majority of the small farm community population were independent entrepreneurs, as against less than 20 percent in the large farm community, where nearly two-thirds were agricultural wage laborers.

—The small farm community in all instances had better community facilities: more schools, more parks, more newspapers, more civic organizations and more churches.

—The small farms community (Dinuba) had twice as many business establishments as the large-farm town (Arvin) and did 61 percent more retail business, especially in household goods and building equipment.

—Physical facilities for community living—paved streets, sidewalks, garbage disposal, sewage disposal and other public services—were far greater in the small-farm community; indeed, in the industrial-farm community some of these facilities were entirely wanting.

It is reasonable to ask whether in fact the size of farms was the essential determinant of these differences—and needless to say, this question was raised. Research under natural conditions cannot produce those perfect controls that a laboratory will provide, and we examined with great care the alternate hypotheses that were put forward by critics of this study. The alternate explanation most frequently argued was that Arvin was much younger than Dinuba. When we plotted the growth of the towns, we found that Arvin was between 20 and 25 years younger, but that the facilities that differentiated the two communities were, in all instances, much older than this differential in age. We also made some comparisons with neighboring towns of Arvin's age where the farms were smaller and these, too, showed a richer local social life than the larger-farm community.

It was part of the original design to engage in a second phase of the study, in which we would investigate all the rural communities in the San Joaquin Valley. Had we been able to do this, and had it supported the comparison between Arvin and Dinuba—as I am confident it would have done—there would have been no question of the cause of the differences between Arvin and Dinuba.

But a powerful pressure against the study developed, spearheaded by the Associated Farmers and picked up by the national press. Pressure was brought to bear on the Bureau of Agricultural Economics, so that its director ordered me to discontinue the investigation after I had completed work on Arvin and Dinuba. The issue took on such magnitude that it was the subject of a detailed historical review. [2]

In the quarter century since the publication of that study, corporate farming has spread to other parts of the country, particularly to the American agricultural heartland which has always been the scene of family-sized commercial farmers. This development has, like so many other events of the period, been assumed to be natural, inevitable and progressive, and little attention has been paid to the costs that have been incurred. I do not mean the costs in money, or in subventions inequitably distributed to large farmers. I mean the costs in the traditions of our society and its rural institutions.

Recently it was suggested that I examine our research with the perspective of twenty-five years, and in the process I have reread my works and some of the controversy they engendered. I am satisfied that the canons of scientific inquiry were scrupulously followed, that the data are clear and unequivocal, and the analysis is basically sound. It is important to emphasize that the analysis rests firmly on well-established sociological theory, and I want to comment briefly on these theoretical matters.

The thesis of the study is that industrialized farming creates an urban pattern of social organization. Urban social orders, unlike rural ones, are characterized by social heterogeneity, social class, depersonalized social relationships which are dominated by pecuniary considerations rather than sentimental ties, and increased differentials of power leading to alienation and apathy in the mass population.

In California we had created a new kind of agriculture, based upon extensive holdings, heavy mechanization and capitalization, and above all on the existence of a large class of laborers. Thus the essentials of industrial production, which have characterized urban economic activities since the industrial revolution, were introduced into the rural landscape, and with them went the elements of urban social life.

With these theoretical considerations in mind, we can return to the comparison between Arvin and Dinuba. Clearly the study revealed precisely those differences that are expressed in the theory of urbanization: increased differentials in social status and class distinctions, impoverishment, the absence of social ties based upon sentiment and the substitution of wages instead, a general lack of participation in the social system by the majority of the people, and a sense of alienation among them. Under these circumstances, it is hardly possible for me to doubt the validity of the research, not merely as a description of the events and circumstances it sets forth, but in the broader implications for the future of rural life in America. Let me conclude by discussing these implications.

If the production of agricultural goods is to become increasingly large-scale and corporation-dominated, rural communities as we have known them will cease to exist. Instead, the landscape will be dotted by what can be called company towns, made up of workers and overseers, together with such service personnel as the company chooses not to provide itself. Lacking any orientation to community and other sense of social belonging, the farmworker will find his interests increasingly identified with his union. In fact the absentee and corporate owners will favor the unions because they will find, as industrialists readily do, that this makes for easier management.

This matter of unionization requires some special attention. The larger growers have fought unionization in the past and have profited by the low level of wages. This has, in turn, been very hard on the small farmer, for a large proportion of his income derives from his own and his family's labor. It is an ironic fact that the early introduction of unionized labor would have helped to protect the small farm system, but that unionization has begun to take hold only after the invasion of the agricultural scene by giant corporations. The irony is compounded by the fact that small farmers have, because of deeply felt ties to the concept of independence, generally been opposed to the unions.

American society was built on the assumption that the population would consist largely of independent entrepreneurs, artisans, self-employed professionals and, above all, independent farmers. Industrialization has effectively eroded this concept for urban populations. The independent family farmer has been an important leaven, preserving that quintessential independence of spirit that has characterized American culture. The study of Arvin and Dinuba has shown what effect corporate and large-scale control can have on rural community life. The vision of the future under increased corporate control of the land is the vision of Arvins rather than Dinubas—indeed of super-Arvins.

Is this an inevitable development? Is it possible that there is no stemming the tide of an evolution toward corporate control of agriculture? There is no real evidence that this is the case. Government policies with respect to tax laws, agricultural subsidies and farm labor have been potent forces affecting the growth of large-scale and corporate farming. This growth cannot therefore be said to be natural; it is the result of force-feeding, of the injection of fiscal hormones, if you will. If the growth of corporate farming can be force-fed, so too can the time-honored traditions of American life.

[1] Walter Goldschmidt, *Small Business and the Community: A Study of Farm Operations.* Report of the Special Committee to Study Problems of American Small Business. The U.S. Senate, (79th Congress; 2nd Session). U.S. Government Printing Office, Washington, D.C. December 23, 1946.

[2] Richard S. Kirkendall, "Social Sciences in the Central Valley: An Episode." *The California Historical Society Quarterly,* 1964.

They're Destroying our Small Towns

What is the psychological impact of a large absentee-owned farm on the residents of a small rural town? Victor K. Ray went to Odebolt, Iowa, to find out, and produced this beautifully written report.

—————————————————————————— *Victor K. Ray*

Odebolt is in western Iowa, in an area that has been blessed with rich soil and good weather. A drought comes only about every twenty years—in 1936 and 1956, folks recall—and then only for a year at a time.

The town is centrally located in the triangle of Omaha, Sioux Falls, Des Moines. Temperatures in January average about nineteen degrees, immobilizing the organic matter that makes the soil dark and rich, and it rises to an average of seventy-four degrees in July. The last killing frost ordinarily comes about May 4 and the first killing frost in the fall comes about October 2. Extremes can go above a hundred degrees in the summer and well below zero in the winter. The average growing season is an ideal 151 days; average rainfall is thirty inches a year.

The land rolls gently, lending itself to full cultivation; the topography is kinder than the river bluffs area to the west. Houses sit squarely, conservatively, tending to face straight east, south, west or north. The architectural angles are modest squares, rectangles, and safely peaked roofs. Many of the houses are two-story, with one-story lean-to additions to accommodate growing families. Barns are rugged, painted against the extremes of weather, many with hay fork-supporting hip roofs.

A sign at the outskirts says that Odebolt is the "Star in the Crown of Iowa." Nearby is an extraordinarily neat cemetery, noticeably well cared for in this state which seems to care for its dead with unusual reverence.

There is a comfortable, intimate triteness about the business district. A story of one Iowa town tells of the theater owner who built a new movie palace, with a red carpet out to the sidewalk. When it was finished, attendance declined. In desperation, he hired a consultant to find out why. It was the red carpet. Folks didn't feel comfortable coming in off the street, with their dusty shoes, stepping on the fine red carpet. Attendance was restored when the carpet was removed.

It is easy to believe that it could have happened in Odebolt. The people of Odebolt are too considerate to track dirt into a neighbor's home or business, or to complain at the absence of a foot scraper at the door, or about a pretentious thick carpet inside.

There are things not visible in the prosaic facade or neat, proud homes that sit along the tree-covered streets of Odebolt; shadows not apparent in the enormous elms that cool the lawns and churchyards; messages not communicated by a hurrying housewife stewing along on an errand or the businessman crossing the empty street to the bank for his daily deposit.

But there is a subject they discuss among themselves. It is something that angers, confuses, makes them envious, and saddens them. The topic is Shinrone Farms, Inc., 6,000 acres that surround the town on the south and west sides. It sits there, always visible, dominating the heart and mind, choking off the bloodstream and pride of the community, showing to the people of Odebolt every day of the year the presence of an invader of their way of life. The wealth of its owners seduces the youngsters. Its presence robs businessmen of hope for the future. It hovers there, its headquarters spreading away at the end of a mile-and-a-half tunnel of road lined and covered by magnificent elms that meet high above its center. But even the elms are sick, as though made ill by a contagion of the invader. The trees betray their illness in a telltale white substance that streaks down the trunks, the deadly symptom of Dutch Elm disease. When they are gone, Shinrone will be even more visible to the town.

It was the Adams Ranch, and is still called that despite its recent new ownership and its interesting new name. Odeboltians look at the gleaming white tractors and combines and other farm equipment—$250,000 worth, according to the *Des Moines Register*—and see in the green shamrock on the radiators the flag of an alien force. The farm equipment was not bought locally. A businessman says with some bitterness that it was bought direct from the manufacturer, although a dealer at the county seat, Sac City, may be involved "in order to service the equipment."

The new owner is William Oldfield Bridge, whom few citizens of Odebolt have seen. He has a sentimentality about Ireland, as the shamrocks attest. Bridge is a Detroit trucking executive, operating a vast automobile hauling agency, the Baker Driveaway Company.

They say that Bridge and his wife may move to Odebolt and, if they do, it will be a most natural choice. For this beautiful community and its friendly people must be a temptation to a family accustomed to the ugly roar and impersonal grind of Detroit. It must be better to live in Odebolt than even in the spacious suburb of Bloomfield Hills, Michigan, where the papers say the Bridges now reside. Besides, Bridge is interested in horses, the newspapers say, and Shinrone will be glamorized by the presence of fine horses.

It is doubtful that anyone in Odebolt will convey to the Bridges what a barrier they must surmount if they are to find the natural friendliness they expect. It is unlikely that a single resident of this considerate little city will speak frankly with these strangers. Indeed, there are few who would like to face their own hostile feelings in the matter, for those who have met Bridge say that he seems to be a decent sort, friendly and sociable.

But implacable history must be overcome for the Bridges to find welcome in Odebolt. The Adams Ranch has a wall around it—scar tissue that has hardened in response to its alien presence in this area where families have farmed their own land, their children have grown up together, visited in each other's homes, gone to the same churches, shared the same pleasures, dissatisfactions and tedium of lonesome days, and have longed for the adventure of life.

The character of the Adamses has been dimmed in the rushing years that have included wars and disasters and murders. Some of the older folks remember. William Adams was "a pretty good man," they recall, "known and respected in the town." Somehow he managed to buy the land around the turn of the century from somebody who had acquired it for $3 an acre or less from a railroad. Then the Adams' name is further confused by the fact that three generations came and went. William Adams' son, Robert, was an odd one, they say. "He wanted to buy the whole town," somebody says.

"You mean, literally, he wanted to *buy* the town?" you ask.

"Well, it was the same thing. He said that if folks would rename the town 'Adamsville,' he would pave the streets."

They turned him down.

Then there was the time an Adams (was it Robert, or his son, William II?) made a deal with the local elevator to sell some corn. On the day it was to be delivered, a disastrous storm covered the roads and the trees and the streets with a sheet of ice. There was conversation with the elevator manager who said, "Bring the corn another day."

"No, we've got a deal. We'll deliver it today."

Then, they say Adams ordered his hired hands—who would have liked to be in by the fire on such a day—to haul manure from the barnlots and spread it on the road to town so the loads of grain could be delivered. Inevitably the ice melted, but the manure—and its odor—remained and spread across the town, insulting the people. It was as if Adams had made a statement to the town, letting them know his contempt.

A new pastor arrived and observed the bitterness. When William Adams II walked down the street, nobody spoke. The pastor met him one morning and said, "Good morning, Mr. Adams." The young man just looked the other way.

The most recent owner before the Bridges was Charles Lakin. He mixed with farmers and bought some things locally. His wife was a member of St. Martin's Catholic Church.

But among the first things you will hear about Lakin was that he received $241,000 in payments under the Agricultural Stabilization and Conservation Service program in 1966. "What right has a millionaire got receiving that kind of payment from the government?" they ask.

Mostly, Odebolt hides its shame from the world. But among themselves they talk about it. In fact, it seems "they talk about nothing else," somebody said. And now other farms are consolidating; other acreages are growing. They see it all as a part of the materialism that seems to obsess the new America.

Father Linus Eisenbacher of St. Martin's Church is a short man with a pock-marked face and a rounding middle. Despite his name, he seems to speak in an Irish accent.

He tells the story of St. Martin's, named for St. Martin of Tours, a soldier who became disgusted with war. One day he met a beggar and cut his cloak in two, giving half to the beggar and, in a dream that night, he saw that the beggar was actually the Lord. He was made a saint for his vision.

Father Eisenbacher can appreciate the idealism of St. Martin. "The whole thing," he says, meaning the pressures that are taking people off the farms, "is affecting our people adversely. People are money hungry. They are secular. Spiritual values have gone down the drain.

"Rural people live close to God," he continues. "The rain and the sunshine and the good weather. The farmer is reminded every day that he is dependent on God. But people who draw a salary don't care about such things. They just begin to live at night.

"I was born and raised on a farm. You could tell something about the season just by looking. There was the thunder and lightning with the storms. Here, even in this little town, you can't see a storm until it's on you."

St. Martin's has had a 30 to 50 percent drop in participation of its members in the seven years Father Eisenbacher has been there. "Religious attitudes are directly related to the land," he said.

"The small farmer can't compete," he added bitterly. "The government doesn't do a thing for the small farmer."

And now William Oldfield Bridge has bought Shinrone, hoping, perhaps, to find the peace that comes from walking in the plowed ground, involving oneself in the processes of creation. But he arrived at the wrong time in history at a place already ruined, and he arrived under the wrong circumstances.

The whole matter came to the attention of his neighbors-to-be on March 17, 1968, when the *Des Moines Sunday Register* carried a story on Shinrone, Inc. that dominated the front page of its farm section. The story told of a shipment of new machinery coming to Shinrone:

"Folks blink a bit in this community at the sight of snow-white farm tractors, combines, implements and the like—all painted this somewhat unusual (for farm equipment) color. The white machinery is a part of the new look at what once was the 'Adams Ranch,' then the 'Lakin Ranch' and is now Shinrone Farms. There will be about $250,000 worth of such white-painted farm tractors, combines, and equipment brought to the famous Sac County farming spread."

The story went on to identify Bridge and tell of the history of the farm, pointing out that it had sold to Lakin in 1962 for an estimated $2.5 million, and that Lakin had received payments from the U.S. Department of Agriculture in 1966 amounting to $241,000, more than anybody else in Iowa. The story said that Bridge had visited Shinrone three or four times.

If folks in Odebolt were blinking at the big equipment purchase, their eyes really popped open three days later when the *Des Moines Register* returned to Shinrone and William O. Bridge. The paper printed a lengthy Associated Press story datelined Washington by Harry Rosenthal and Gaylord Shaw. The headline was an attention-getter: "He settles $594,398 Tax For $110,000."

The story quoted Harry Snyder, chief of the Internal Revenue Service collection division, about how the IRS had decided to settle for less than 20 percent of its claim. "If I were a gambling man, I would bet we got all we can," said Snyder.

The article continued:

"On October 10, at 2:40 p.m. an official memorandum and notice of the sale of the Lakin Ranch to Shinrone, Inc. was filed with June Rheinfrank, Sac County, Iowa, recorder.

"Shinrone took possession of the ranch on March 1. Sale price was not disclosed, but an expert on land values estimated the farm is worth $3 million or more. He based this on the going price for farmland in Sac County, $500 to $700 an acre."

The AP story went on the quote the IRS examiner as saying that Bridge did not own any property, that it was all in his wife's name.

Odebolt folks were interested to read that the Bridges have a number of corporations and that their home in Bloomfield Hills is on a 50-acre plot, assessed for tax purposes at $147,000. Frances Bridge was listed as the owner. The IRS examiner said that Bridge told him his assets were only $100 cash and a life insurance policy with a surrender value of $10,668.

It was a sobering story to the folks of Odebolt, most of whom work hard for their money and who have never thought of contesting the Internal Revenue Service and have never, in their most unrestrained dreams, visualized owning a $3 million ranch.

The People Left Behind

In 1967, President Lyndon B. Johnson appointed a distinguished commission to study the subject of rural poverty. Edward T. Breathitt, former governor of Kentucky, was named chairman. After many months of hearings and field investigations, the commission issued a comprehensive report, The People Left Behind, *that stands as a shameful indictment of America's neglect of its rural population.*

The following summary of the commission's findings is taken from its 1967 report. Four years later, when Governor Breathitt testified before the Senate Subcommittee on Migratory Labor, he was asked if things had gotten better in the interim. ''Nothing much has changed,'' he replied.

— *The President's Commission on Rural Poverty*

This report is about a problem which many in the United States do not realize exists. The problem is rural poverty. It affects some 14 million Americans. Rural poverty is so widespread, and so acute, as to be a national disgrace, and its consequences have swept into our cities, violently.

The urban riots during 1967 had their roots, in considerable part, in rural poverty. A high proportion of the people crowded into city slums today came there from rural slums. This fact alone makes clear how large a stake the people of this nation have in an attack on rural poverty.

The total number of rural poor would be even larger than 14 million had not so many of them moved to the city. They made the move because they wanted a job and a decent place to live. Some have found them. Many have not. Many merely exchanged life in a rural slum for life in an urban slum, at exorbitant cost to themselves, to the cities, and to rural America as well.

Even so, few migrants have returned to the rural areas they left. They have apparently concluded that bad as conditions are in an urban slum, they are worse in the rural slum they fled from.

Our programs for rural America are woefully out of date.

Some of our rural programs, especially farm and vocational agriculture programs, are relics from an earlier era. They were developed in a period during which the welfare of farm families was equated with the well-being of rural communities and of all rural people. This is no longer so.

They were developed without anticipating the vast changes in technology, and the consequences of this technology to rural people. Instead of combating low incomes of rural people, these programs have helped to create wealthy landowners while largely bypassing the rural poor.

Most rural programs still do not take the speed and consequences of technological change into account. We have not yet adjusted to the fact that in the brief period of fifteen years, from 1950 to 1965, new machines and new methods increased farm output in the United States by 45 percent—and reduced farm employment 45 percent. Nor is there adequate awareness that during the next fifteen years the need for farm labor will decline by another 45 percent. Changes like these on the farm are paralleled on a broader front throughout rural America, affecting many activities other than farming and touching many more rural people than those on farms.

In contrast to the urban poor, the rural poor, notably the white, are not well organized, and have few spokesmen for bringing the nation's attention to their problems. The more vocal and better organized urban poor gain most of the benefits of current antipoverty programs.

Until the past few years, the nation's major social welfare and labor legislation largely bypassed rural Americans, especially farmers and farmworkers. Farm people were excluded from the Social Security Act until the mid-1950s. Farmers, farmworkers and workers in agriculturally related occupations are still excluded from other major labor legislation, including the unemployment insurance programs, the Labor-Management Relations Act, the Fair Labor Standards Act, and most state workmen's compensation acts.

Because we have been oblivious of the rural poor, we have abetted both rural and urban poverty, for the two are closely linked through migration. The hour is late for taking a close look at rural poverty, gaining an understanding of its consequences and developing programs for doing something about it. The Commission is unanimous in the conviction that effective programs for solving the problems of rural poverty will contribute to the solution of urban poverty as well.

The facts of rural poverty are summarized in the paragraphs that follow.

Rural poverty in the United States has no geographic boundaries. It is acute in the South, but it is present and serious in the East, the West and the North. Rural poverty is not limited to Negroes. It permeates all races and ethnic groups. Nor is poverty limited to the farm. Our farm population has declined until it is only a small fraction of our total rural population. Most of the rural poor do not live on farms. They live in the open country, in rural villages and in small towns. Moreover, contrary to a common misconception, whites outnumber nonwhites among the rural poor by a wide margin. It is true, however, that an extremely high proportion of Negroes in the rural South and Indians on reservations are destitute.

Hunger, even among children, does exist among the rural poor, as a group of physicians discovered recently in a visit to the rural South. They found Negro children not getting enough food to sustain life, and so disease ridden as to be beyond cure. Malnutrition is even more widespread. The evidence appears in bad diets and in diseases which often are a product of bad diets.

Disease and premature death are startlingly high among the rural poor. Infant mortality, for instance, is far higher among the rural poor than among the least privileged group in urban areas. Chronic diseases also are common among both young and old. And medical and dental care is conspicuously absent.

Unemployment and underemployment are major problems in rural America. The rate of unemployment nationally is about 4 percent. The rate in rural areas averages about 18 percent. Among farmworkers, a recent study discovered that underemployment runs as high as 37 percent.

The rural poor have gone, and now go, to poor schools. One result is that more than 3 million rural adults are classified as illiterates. In both educational facilities and opportunities, the rural poor have been shortchanged.

Most of the rural poor live in atrocious houses. One in every 13 houses in rural America is officially classified as unfit to live in.

Many of the rural poor live in chronically depressed poverty-stricken rural communities. Most of the rural South is one vast poverty area. Indian reservations contain heavy concentrations of poverty. But there also are impoverished rural communities in the upper Great Lakes region, in New England, in Appalachia, in the Southwest and in other sections.

The community in rural poverty areas has all but disappeared as an effective institution. In the past the rural community performed the services needed by farmers and other rural people. Technological progress brought sharp declines in the manpower needs of agriculture, forestry, fisheries and mining. Other industries have not replaced the jobs lost, and they have supplied too few jobs for the young entries in the labor market. Larger towns and cities have taken over many of the economic and social functions of the villages and small towns.

The changes in rural America have rendered obsolete many of the political boundaries to villages and counties. Thus these units operate on too small a scale to be practicable. Their tax base has eroded as their more able-bodied wage earners left for jobs elsewhere. In consequence the public services in the typical poor rural community are grossly inadequate in number, magnitude and quality. Local government is no longer able to cope with local needs.

As the communities ran downhill, they offered fewer and fewer opportunities for anyone to earn a living. The inadequately equipped young people left in search of better opportunities elsewhere. Those remaining behind have few resources with which to earn incomes adequate for a decent living and for revitalizing their communities.

For all practical purposes, then, most of the 14 million poor people in rural areas are outside our market economy. So far as they are concerned, the dramatic economic growth of the United States might as well never have happened. It has brought them few rewards. They are on the outside looking in, and they need help.

Congress and state legislatures from time to time have enacted many laws and appropriated large sums of money to aid the poverty-stricken and to help rural America. Very little of the legislation or the money has helped the rural poor. Major farm legislation directed at commercial farms has been successful in helping farmers adjust supply to demand, but it has not helped farmers whose production is very small. And because the major social welfare and labor legislation has discriminated against rural people, many of the rural poor—farmers and farmworkers particularly—have been denied unemployment insurance, denied the right of collective bargaining and denied the protection of workmen's compensation laws.

This Commission questions the wisdom of massive public efforts to improve the lot of the poor in our central cities without comparable efforts to meet the needs of the poor in rural America. Unfortunately, as public programs improve the lot of the urban poor, without making similar improvements in conditions for the rural poor, they provide fresh incentive for the rural poor to migrate to the central cities. The only solution is a coordinated attack on both urban and rural poverty.

The Commission is convinced that the abolition of rural poverty in the United States, perhaps for the first time in any nation, is completely feasible. The nation has the economic resources and the technical means for doing this. What it has lacked, thus far, has been the will. The Commission rejects the view that poverty, in so rich a nation, is inevitable for any large group of its citizens.

The Future
of Rural Policy

*As director of the Office of Economic Opportunity's economic devel-
opment program during the late 1960s, Geoffrey Faux was actively
involved in what he now calls ''band aid'' efforts to aid rural America. The
so-called War on Poverty failed to accomplish much in rural America,
Faux concluded, because it didn't go to the root of the problem: maldis-
tribution of land, wealth and power. Here, in testimony before the Senate
Migratory Labor Subcommittee, Faux explains why current policies toward
rural America have reached a dead end, and why a new approach—land
reform—is necessary.*

Geoffrey Faux

Public policy towards rural poverty is at a dead end. The
"depressed areas" programs of the Economic Development
Administration for the most part have become pork barrels with
little space in the bottom for any social or economic change. The
programs of the Department of Agriculture are operated for the
benefit of agribusiness and state politicians. And the programs of
HEW, OEO and the Labor Department have consistently
shortchanged the rural poor, primarily because there is no
political constituency for them.

The conventional solution to the plight of the rural poor is
the "welfare/mobility" strategy. It holds that since there are not
enough jobs in rural areas, the rural poor must leave for places
where work prospects are better. Therefore, public policy
supports the outmigration of the poor to areas where jobs are
growing. Since outmigration is happening anyway, this means an
acceleration of present trends, rather than a new policy. For
those who do not choose to migrate, the "mobility/welfare"
strategy provides welfare, at least in theory.

So-called "growth center" strategies, whereby subsidies are

given to accelerate growth in already growing small urban areas, are supplements to the mobility/welfare design. At best, the net effect of this approach is to divert some small amount of rural-to-urban migration away from the large cities to smaller ones.

A mobility strategy without much welfare is in fact the strategy that the nation is pursuing now. It is a strategy that systematically squeezes the rural poor so that their choice more and more is between migration and misery.

It is not surprising that bureaucrats and economists seek to solve the problem by accelerating present trends. Given the existing distribution of economic power, the poor are increasingly irrelevant to the technological requirements of rural industry and, almost by definition, moving should give them a better chance to improve their earning power and productivity. For bureaucrats, the rural poor offer the least political resistance and therefore are selected to bear the burden of stabilizing the rural economy. For economists, the existing distribution of power is always a "given."

The mobility strategy has dominated the allocation of resources in the war on poverty. But it certainly does not reflect a unanimous view. Those who worked in rural areas or who took enough time out from shuffling papers to go into the countryside saw that the neat solution worked out in Washington made little sense in the Mississippi Delta, eastern Kentucky or south Texas. They found that:

—A substantial number of the poor do not leave rural areas.

—The rural poor are not necessarily better off when driven to urban areas where they have no skills, can find no jobs and have great difficulty adjusting to the city culture.

—The human cost of such forced migration is very high.

—Because of these high costs of migration, a substantial number of the poor will not leave the countryside until forced to do so by hunger and extreme deprivation. In the country they can supplement their income with a garden, in some areas by hunting and fishing, and, perhaps most important, with a network of family and neighbors which is the backbone of rural life.

—Contrary to popular assumption, there are economic opportunities in rural areas. In some cases there are industrial opportunities, in some cases farming opportunities, and in a growing number of areas there are rapidly rising opportunities in recreation and tourism.

—Tax policies, direct and indirect subsidies and technical aid programs systematically exclude the poor.

—The mobility strategy is encouraging the concentration of ownership and power in the hands of fewer and fewer private interests. And as economic power concentrates, so does political power, so that local officials in rural areas speak for the powerful and the rich and oppose even "band-aid" OEO programs if they can't control them.

—Concentrated ownership is becoming absentee ownership, weakening any sense of responsibility that landowners might have for their less fortunate neighbors.

An example of how antipoverty policies ignored reality was the rural loan program authorized by Title III-A of the Economic Opportunity Act. The rural loan program was set up to provide financial assistance to low-income farm families and farmers' cooperatives. The program was poorly designed from the beginning. It was then delegated to the Farmer's Home Administration which proceeded to disregard the intent of the program to help the rural poor. Thus, the General Accounting Office found that despite the desperate need of poor farmers for technical assistance, the Farmer's Home Administration gave substantially *less* help to poor farmers than to middle class and rich farmers. The poor were left to rely on their own resources and skills, while the wealthy were supported by a government agency.

Despite this and other evidence that the program had been mishandled, OEO decided that the notion of federal aid to poor farmers had "failed" and agreed with the Bureau of the Budget that the loan program should be dropped. This meant that a revolving fund with almost $100 million worth of assets, generated out of previous years' appropriations and the repayments of poor farmers, was sent back to the Treasury. Thus, money that poor farmers are paying back to the government is available for loans and subsidies to the rich.

A number of attempts have been made to help rural poor people gain some ownership and some economic power, though these scattered efforts can hardly be called a program. Projects were of shapes and sizes; catfish farming in Georgia and Mississippi and Alabama, cattle raising in Mississippi and New Mexico, light industrial enterprises in Minnesota, West Virginia and South Carolina.

These projects have made great strides, but there is still a long way to go. Not only do they not get the technical aid from the federal government that wealthy farmers and corporations get, but there is no rational system of financing available. Agribusiness of course has its own form of financing. And rich farmers and their cooperatives get plenty of financial support from the Department of Agriculture. But the poor are effectively cut off from such aid, both individually and when they attempt to band together in cooperatives.

Where do we go from here? How do we get out of the dead end into which our rural policies have taken us?

The first step is to recognize the nature of the issue. Behind the "problems" of bad housing, poor education, insufficient jobs, lack of capital to start a business and so on, is a system of unequal distribution of land and resources under a largely absentee ownership. This system has been created by tax policies, subsidy programs and technical aid efforts paid for by the U.S. taxpayer.

If there has been a broad survey of corporate land ownership in the United States, I am unaware of it. However, in my own limited observations, many of the same corporate names seem to crop us in different parts of the country. Among the major corporate landowners in Maine are Georgia Pacific, the International Paper Company and St. Regis Paper. In Harlan County, Kentucky, the largest landowners in the county are U.S. Steel, International Paper and Georgia Pacific. In Jefferson County, Mississippi, the largest landowners are Johns Manville, International Paper and St. Regis Paper.

This concentration of power renders helpless not just the poor but all parts of rural society. Even where skillful men of good intent lead a local government, they cannot make the changes needed because rural communities themselves are in bondage to corporate powers. And it is not in the nature of things for International Paper to tax itself for better housing in Maine, or for Georgia Pacific to concern itself with schools in Harlan County, Kentucky, or for St. Regis to worry about poor black sharecroppers in Jefferson County, Mississippi.

The next step is to develop a strategy for rural development that concentrates on helping those who need help. Elements in such a strategy might include:

—Credit, training and technical assistance for poor people's cooperatives and self-help enterprises.

—Reform of farm subsidy programs which favor corporate giants over the small farmer.

—Extension of minimum wage laws to farm workers.

—A shift in agricultural research from large-scale technology suitable for smaller farms.

—Reform of tax policies which encourage the wealthy to speculate in land.

—A land bank in which the federal government finances purchase of land for locally-owned enterprises. Like the urban renewal program, the rural land bank would provide land value "write-downs." Unlike the urban renewal program, projects would be sponsored and owned by local or regional development corporations responsible to the communities involved. Through these development corporations, migrant workers could be given an opportunity to settle and obtain land ownership.

—Comprehensive land reform through both legal and legislative action.

It is not easy to conclude that an important part of the solution to rural poverty is in the redistribution of land. Such a solution seems to lie so far into the future, and each day that goes by is another day of suffering for migrants and other rural people. But after seven years of trying to cure poverty with band-aids, we cannot continue to delude ourselves as to the real nature of the disease.

Ironically, the United States has been preaching the virtues of land reform to less-developed countries since the end of World War II. The forces that resist land reform in Latin America and Asia are similar to the forces that have prevented it from becoming a subject of serious discussion in this country. But for better or worse, land reform is as much a key to the elimination of rural poverty in America as it is anywhere else on the globe.

T. L. Gettings. *Pennsylvania, 1973.*

Bob Fitch. *Corporate management of farmland for investors; California.*

Bob Griffith. *Abandoned farmhouse, Pennsylvania, 1973.*

Larger and fewer farms and absentee ownership

USDA. *Co-Op-owned grain elevator, sixty-seven feet short of a half-mile long; Kansas, 1961.*

Russell Lee, FSA. *Agricultural ghost town; Oklahoma, 1939.*

T. L. Gettings. *Working a field; Pennsylvania, 1974.*

...drain the life from the rural community.

USDA. *Haymond, Kentucky, 1965.*

Walker Evans, FSA. *Advance, Alabama, 1936.*

USDA. *Poor family in their living room; Georgia, 1965.*

USDA. *Playing in the yard; Georgia, 1965.*

USDA. *Chicano home; Texas, 1967.*

Mike Jennings. *Urban slum; Pennsylvania, 1971.*

*The only escape for the rural poor is to
the urban slum.*

Russell Lee, FSA. *Abandoned store; Minnesota, 1937.*

Part VII:
Co-Ops, Land Trusts and Land Reform

The Poor People's Co-Ops

In this final section, we look at some alternatives to corporate domination of rural America and consider ways to build them.

One alternative is the cooperative. There are, of course, many types of cooperatives: food co-ops, housing co-ops, electric co-ops, credit unions and so on. Of particular interest is the farm cooperative in which independent farmers pool their resources and labor to attain economies that would not be available to them separately. As land and capital costs rise, cooperatives of this type are important as a way for low-income people to get started as self-employed farmers.

There are scores of low-income farm cooperatives now operating in different parts of the United States. One of the most successful has been the Cooperativa Campesina *in Watsonville, California, which reporter Nick Kotz describes in the following article. Kotz's story originally appeared in the* Washington Post *on October 5, 1971, when the co-op was just getting started. In the intervening years, the co-op's annual sales have climbed to $1.1 million, and the net cash income of its member families has risen to $14,000. The S. S. Pierce Company, mentioned in the article as a nearby corporate competitor, has gone out of the strawberry business.*

Nick Kotz

Tereso Morales has struggled all his life at the bottom of the richest agricultural system in history. Since he was nine years old, he has stooped in fields from Oregon to Texas, harvesting wealth owned by big farmers, retail food chains, canners and agribusiness conglomerates.

Morales, 35, is still breaking his back in the fields, but with new purpose. His mind is now fired with a dream of sharing in some of the riches of American agriculture. He has joined with thirty other migrant workers and small farmers to grow strawberries in Watsonville, California. He hopes to earn $10,000 a year to raise his eleven-member family in some place other than a labor camp or a big city slum.

The thirty-one families of *Cooperativa Campesina* in many

203

ways symbolize the problems and aspirations of 13 million poor rural Americans.

The cooperative movement may give some of these people a way out of poverty. But the odds on their success are small.

They are competing—as are family farmers—against powerful, efficient and aggressive agribusiness corporations that have moved into American agriculture on a large scale.

Morales and the other families of *Cooperativa Campesina*, for example, are competing in the California strawberry market with Tenneco, a $4.3 billion conglomerate, and with S.S. Pierce Co., which both grows and distributes its own brand of premium-priced foods. They are also competing, in a larger sense, with political forces that have shaped federal agricultural policies in ways that favor the largest and most efficient interests in agriculture.

For more than 35 years—to take the most obvious case in point—American industrial workers have been represented by powerful labor unions that have secured minimum wage legislation, unemployment compensation, child labor regulations, workmen's compensation for injuries on the job, collective bargaining rights and so on. Farm workers like Morales generally enjoy none of these rights and benefits.

When the United Farmworkers Organizing Committee, led by Cesar Chavez, sought to achieve some of the same be n efits, government responded by undercutting the movement with policies permitting employers to import cheap labor from Mexico and Puerto Rico. When Chavez and his union sought to gain bargaining rights with a retail boycott of grapes and lettuce, the Defense Department increased its purchases of grapes and lettuce.

At the same time, the government has continued its subsidies to large farm operations through the provision of low-cost irrigation water, the development of labor-displacing machinery and generous tax laws.

The domination of what is left of rural America by agribusiness corporations is not only accelerating the migration patterns of recent decades but raises the spectre of a kind of twentieth century agricultural feudalism in the culture that remains.

In response to this vision of the future, the federal government in the 1960s undertook limited measures to stimulate the survival of small farms and small towns. The anti-poverty programs administered by the Office of Economic Opportunity touched the problem in certain ways.

Tereso Morales, for example, learned to read and write in an adult education course sponsored by OEO for migrant workers. He learned, too, that he and other farm laborers might earn a living growing high-value fruits and vegetables. So he persuaded three of his OEO classmates to join him in putting up $500 apiece to launch *Cooperativa Campesina,* with Morales as president.

Working from sun-up to dark in the co-op's 140-acre leased fields, Morales has little time or patience to talk with visitors about abstractions. He is laying several miles of irrigation pipe and supervising the leveling of irrigation ditches. It is an exacting job. If the irrigation troughs vary by more than one inch in 100 feet, water may slop over and mildew the strawberries.

The dream or heartbreak at the end of this labor will come next year. If all goes well, each acre of strawberries should produce gross sales of about $9,000. Then the cooperative will find out whether corporate competitors attempt to frustrate its marketing plans.

"In a good year I could earn $5,000 as a migrant," relates Morales, "but that means travelling for twelve solid months. It's very hard on the family. How are you going to do that and raise nine kids, send them to school, give them a chance? You can't keep running forever. I'm not moving anymore."

The coordination of cooperative farming is no easy matter, and has produced some failures. *Cooperativa Campesina* divides up land and profits on the basis of family size and family contributions to work. Its members so far are sticking together.

"We want to benefit our community and do all we can to exist," says Morales. "Our members are not afraid to work. With what we have to go back to, this looks pretty good."

The co-op got started with a $100,000 loan from an OEO-funded consulting firm and a $150,000 loan from the Wells Fargo Bank. When local growers tried to block the loan, a local Wells Fargo official reportedly told them: "You'll take your money out of the bank, but they'll burn the bank down. What am I supposed to do?"

Despite indirect assistance from OEO, the federal government—and particularly the agriculture department—has done little to assist Morales' co-op and similar ones that have been started by blacks in the South and whites in Appalachia.

The Farmers Home Administration turned down *Cooperativa Campesina's* request for a loan. "The low-income farmer problem is not personally my cup of tea," says Homer Preston, deputy administrator of USDA's Farmer Cooperative Service. "Our conventional co-ops are not exactly enthusiastic about them. They don't have much to offer except labor and it is less important today. These people were cotton choppers. They're tied in with idealism and civil rights, and a lot of romanticism. The purpose of cooperatives is not to keep mass numbers in farming but to help those who remain. You can't go against market trends when everything else points to bigness."

In the course of assisting "bigness", Preston says the FCS is helping merger negotiations between the country's two largest dairy "super co-ops," which between them control about 40 percent of the milk supply.

When he came to Washington seeking management training assistance for 100 low-income Southern co-ops, says Father A. J. McKnight, FCS advised him to seek help from a private foundation. "The USDA programs have favored the big commercial farmers and have deliberately tried to eliminate the small family farm," said McKnight, referring to research sponsored by the agriculture department and land grant colleges. At a time when poor Southerners are starting to earn a living growing labor-intensive specialty crops like okra, tomatoes, sweet potatoes and cucumbers, McKnight said, USDA is developing strains of the same vegetables which can be harvested mechanically.

Similarly, government-backed research at the University of California is developing a tougher variety of strawberry—with a primary emphasis not on flavor or nutrition, but on its ability to be shipped and picked by machine.

"When I asked about the effects of that strawberry on migrant workers," says Alfred Navarro, a consultant to *Cooperativa Campesina,* "the Extension Service guy said: 'All I worry about is the economic part of it. Let the sociologists worry about that.'

"Mechanization is a fact of life, but the field worker can't get the machine. Who deals with the social effect of these machines? The agriculture department has got to be responsive to more than one sector of the rural economy."

The Prosperous Co-Ops

The cooperative movement in rural America goes back a long way. Here, Richard Margolis looks at some of the history and discusses a haunting dilemma: sometimes, to survive, cooperatives must become big businesses, but in doing so they lose many of the virtues that set them off from large corporations in the first place. Note that the cooperatives Margolis is writing about are different from the Cooperativa Campesina— *they are older, more prosperous, and generally involve established family farmers rather than low-income farmworkers trying to become self-employed farmers.*

The following selection is taken from a longer article on the cooperative movement that appeared in the April 17, 1972 issue of The New Leader.

Richard Margolis———————————————

In 1959 the United States government sent a delegation of farm cooperative experts to India's International Agricultural Fair, hoping they would explain the American cooperative way to all within earshot. One of the delegates was Martin A. Abrahamsen, deputy administrator of the U.S. Farmer Cooperative Service and veteran of many farm co-op struggles. Although the Cold War had not yet begun to thaw, the delegates from behind the Iron Curtain were surprisingly cordial to their American counterparts. "I guess they thought they had more in common with us than they actually did," Abrahamsen recalls.

One Iron Curtain delegate said to Abrahamsen, "We understand your cooperatives. They are socialistic, yes?"

"No," replied Abrahamsen, "they are capitalistic. Cooperatives make better capitalists out of farmers."

After several exchanges of that sort, the Iron Curtain delegates stopped asking questions. But Abrahamsen's response was more than Cold War rhetoric; it reflected the near-unanimous belief among American farmers that strong, competitive co-ops, not Marxist communes, will lead them to the economic Promised Land.

Many small, independent farmers have already vanished from the land, of course, having sold their profitless acres to those new, omnivorous corporations, the minions of agribusiness, which swallow farms the way sharks swallow herring. Since World War II, 30 million Americans have fled the soil.

Of the small farmers who survive, five out of every six families belong to at least one co-op, and a majority belong to three or more. In hundreds of rural towns the local co-op is the one economic bright spot on a prairie of desolation. Consider the Pigeon Falls Co-op Creamery in southeastern Wisconsin.

Founded in 1882, it has somehow managed to weather good times and bad. It now produces about 20,000 pounds of cheese each day on behalf of 215 farmer members, and it employs twenty-five people; in Pigeon Falls (population: 200) this makes it a financial colossus. The co-op is proud of its independence: for ninety years it has resisted mergers with other cooperatives. But according to its president, Arnold Hanson, members "are thinking of joining other milk co-ops in the state." The wonder is that they are only thinking about it. Given the shaky position of small farmers, a local co-op would have to be incredibly stiff-necked not to ally itself with some larger organization.

Yet this raises anew some old ideological questions about the nature of cooperatives. Should a co-op try to become big and powerful, and risk losing touch both with its members and its original purpose? Or should it remain small and personal, and risk losing everything?

Sometimes, there's not much choice. If power (in Lord Acton's sense) corrupts, weakness seems none too useful either. Every farm cooperative has had to learn this lesson. There are fewer farm cooperatives each year, but those that remain tend to grow larger, if not in membership then in the amount of business they do.

In 1922, the peak year in terms of numbers for farm co-ops, nearly 15,000 purchasing and marketing groups grossed under $3 billion; last year, 7,000 cooperatives grossed more than $17 billion. There have been myriad mergers similar to those taking place in other industries, and many of the still-extant independent cooperatives now belong to regional federations that undertake much of the necessary purchasing and marketing on their behalf.

These federations are often slick, sophisticated enterprises—a far cry from the primitive Granges essayed a century ago by people who in many instances could neither read nor write. Gold Kist, Inc. (formerly the Cotton Producers Association) sells supplies to 150,000 members in Georgia, Alabama and elsewhere in the South. Its 1970 gross income from sales of feed, fertilizer and pesticides came to $87 million. To wholesale and consumer markets that year Gold Kist sold eggs, pecans, peanuts, broilers, and other products that brought in nearly $200 million. In addition, Gold Kist owns a loan company, part of an insurance company and at least one foreign subsidiary. In 1969 it returned almost $5 million to co-op members in the form of patronage refunds—*i.e.,* the money farmers had saved by buying supplies and selling produce through the federation.

Gold Kist is not unique. No less than a dozen cooperative conglomerates have balance sheets to rival Gold Kist's, and five are listed among *Fortune's* Top 500. One of these is Farmland Industries, a remarkable federation of 2,000 local co-ops operating in fifteen states across middle America. Like many other successful businesses, Farmland owes some of its growth to its enemies, in this case the petroleum industry.

Farmland began, according to Kenneth S. Davis, a writer and part-time Boswell to the cooperative movement, "as little more than a hopeful gleam in the eye of its president, Howard A. Cowden, a big man with...a sense of mission and a genius for large-scale organization." With the increasingly widespread use of tractors and other farm machinery, Cowden saw the need for a petroleum purchasing co-op. In 1929 he talked six local associations in Kansas into putting up $500 each to start the enterprise, called Union Oil Cooperative. In 1935 the name was changed to the Consumers Cooperative Association, and in 1966 it became Farmland Industries.

The new organization began buying and shipping tank cars of gasoline and tractor fuel directly to its own storage tanks and thence to members. By the end of the first year the number of member associations had grown from six to twenty-two, and each had already received a small rebate in proportion to its purchases. By 1938 the co-op was distributing refined petroleum fuels at the rate of 54 million gallons a year. It was also beginning to worry profit-making competitors in the oil industry. Soon, refineries began cancelling contracts with the federation, threatening, in effect, to cut off its supply of petroleum products. Cowden's response was to spin off a subsidiary, the Cooperative Refinery Association, financed by the sale of $10 shares to cooperating farmers. The new co-op opened a gasoline refinery on New Year's Day, 1940.

Shortly thereafter it began to drill its own oil wells and to install its own pipelines. At each juncture its growth was inadvertently stimulated by the petroleum industry, whose periodic boycotts and embargoes kept forcing the cooperative into new areas of development. Eventually, Farmland owned and operated wells, pipelines, refineries, storage tanks, and trucks—guaranteeing the flow of petroleum products to its members.

In 1947 the industry played its trump card. It instituted a court action challenging the federation's right to manufacture supplies for farmers and sell off such by-products as heavy oil and asphalt to non-farmers. But the Kansas Supreme Court, in a landmark decision, unanimously upheld the co-op. As a Farmland official later observed, "This case pretty well eliminated any question as to the right of a farmer cooperative to integrate vertically its operations"—in other words, not merely to sell supplies to its members, but to manufacture them as well.

Farmland Industries has been "integrating" both vertically and horizontally ever since. Today, besides oil wells and refineries, it owns fertilizer plants, feed mills, factories that produce paint and batteries, a network of warehouses, a fleet of trucks, and two hog slaughtering plants. Its meat sales are the largest of any cooperative in America. In addition, it shares ownership with the Dow Chemical Company in a Missouri agricultural chemicals plant. Farmland has assets approaching $400 million, grosses more than $650 million a year, and provides aid and comfort to 400,000 individual members through their local co-ops. It is a major triumph in economic cooperatism.

Recently I attended Farmland's forty-third annual convention, held in Kansas City's huge municipal auditorium. My first morning I felt I was in the presence of a saving remnant: The farmers kept reminding each other they were alone in a hostile world, sole survivors and keepers of the sacred flame. "Good morning, farmers," boomed the emcee. "It's good to see so many farmers here."

The main speaker that morning was Edward T. Breathitt, former governor of Kentucky and co-chairman of the new Coalition for Rural America. Breathitt said he was working to "preserve the family farm," because "the best values are rooted in rural America." He went on: "One thing is certain. The great American dream resides uneasily in the suburbs of our great cities, while the news media and the policy workers have all but forgotten the hardworking people in rural America.

"Now let me ask you to do me a favor right here and now," Breathitt said. "Stand with me here and let's show *our* appreciation to the hardworking men and women who have the courage to stick it out in American agriculture today. Let's stand here and give them an ovation." Everybody stood up; there was polite applause.

Later, a young man who represented the Future Farmers of America delivered a rousing oration on the importance of leadership. Leadership, he said, didn't come from books; it wasn't born in a person and it wasn't God-given. No, leadership came from "average people."

"You are those people," the young man shouted. "We young people need you now more than ever before."

If there was in the proceeding a note of self-congratulation, one could hardly blame the farmers. The system had done its worst, yet here they were, alive and well in Kansas City. In forty-three years they had collected more than $300 million in savings from their cooperative—not bad in a disappearing industry.

By the time I left the convention, though, I had the impression that the mood in Kansas City was not the mood that had inspired cooperation, nor, indeed, the mood that would *expand* cooperatism. It seemed too self-centered, too enraptured with its own success, to be of much help to newer, younger cooperative impulses. The small farmer who, thanks to his big cooperative, had "stuck it out in agriculture," cared little about bringing the benefits of cooperatism to either his rural neighbor or his urban customer. Rather, he had followed the conventional course of reform movements, from prophets to profits, from ideals to merely "deals."

Many large farm cooperatives have been less than enthusiastic about assisting their poorer rural compatriots— mostly blacks and Chicanos—in *their* cooperative struggles. In fact, several white co-ops in the South have pointedly refused to sell fertilizer to their black counterparts; and on the West Coast some of the larger cooperative growers associations, like Sunkist, have been charged with creating intolerable conditions for Mexican-American farmworkers.

Moreover, some co-ops have closed their doors to new members, failed to keep older members duly informed and, in a few flagrant instances, have even scrapped the one-man, one-vote rule, preferring to parcel out voting power on the basis of each member's selling performance. Briefly put, most farm cooperatives nowadays neither crusade nor proselytize; they mind their own business, and their business is simply...business.

The evolution of the Welch grape juice cooperative tells much of the story. It started in 1869, when Charles Welch, who lived in upstate New York, introduced pasteurized grape juice to the public (and to churches, for use in place of sacramental wine). The business prospered for several generations; but after the Crash of 1929 it began a slow decline, and by the mid-40s' a large block of Welch Company stock was up for grabs.

It was bought by Jacob M. Kaplan, an energetic entrepreneur from New York City who already owned a grape juice processing plant in Brocton, N.Y., near the Welch head-quarters. Kaplan rebuilt the business, stressing aggressive promotion and consistent high quality, and he helped the hard-pressed grape-growers to increase their vineyard yields. Sales and profits zoomed.

But Kaplan, the pragmatic businessman, was also something of a dreamer; he envisioned a cooperative in which grape-growers could further prosper by sharing their savings. In the late '50s, under a pay-as-you-go arrangement, Kaplan turned over the business to his 5,000 grape-growers in New York and six other states. (There was a Welch processing plant in each of the states.) He agreed to remain president without salary while the growers paid him 10 percent of their annual net proceeds toward the agreed-upon purchase price. Once that sum was reached, Kaplan bowed out, and the Welch Grape Juice Company became a full-fledged co-op.

In the ten years since then, the cooperative has broken all sales and earning records. Without doubt it is a huge business success. Yet Kaplan, who now devotes much of his time to running his family foundations in Manhattan, continues to brood over the experiment. He sees the grape-growers becoming narrow and complacent; he is concerned that they do not admit new members to their co-op.

Instead of training and encouraging young people in the cooperative way, complains Kaplan, "they've kept it all for themselves." He fears nearly all agricultural cooperatives are Welching: "They lack vitality and imagination. They are just drifting."

A Land Transfer System

One of the most serious problems faced by family farmers is how to transfer land from one generation to the next. Frequently a farmer must sell his farm to raise money for his retirement, but it's difficult for young people to buy what old farmers sell because land, equipment and credit are so expensive. Consequently, a great deal of family farm land passes into the hands of absentee speculators and corporations.

To deal with this critical problem, the North Dakota Farmers Union Board of Directors has proposed the establishment of a state land transfer system. The NDFU proposal is patterned after the Saskatchewan Land Bank Commission, which for several years has been buying land from retiring farmers and leasing it at low rates to young and low-income farmers. According to its 1973 annual report, the Commission purchased 168,481 acres in 1972-73 from 381 retiring farmers. It leased the land to 425 new farmers whose average age was 34.

North Dakota Farmers' Union

Farm families are finding it increasingly difficult to transfer their farm as an economic unit to the next generation. High interest rates, increasing land values, the lack of sufficient equity and other financial factors have foreclosed many young people from entering agriculture.

After careful review of various land transfer systems, the North Dakota Farmers Union Board of Directors offers the following proposal for transferring land from one generation to the next.

The responsibility for the state's participation in the land transfer system would be vested in a Trust Lands Division. A trust Lands Board would be created to supervise the operation of the Trust Lands Division. Board members would be appointed for staggered terms by the agriculture commissioner.

Any farmer, landowner or estate wishing to transfer land to descendants or to a prospective farmer would sell the land at its

213

appraised agricultural value to the Trust Lands Division.

Financing for the land transfer program would be provided through the Bank of North Dakota. Upon the sale of farm land to the Trust Lands Division, the landowner's descendant would have first option to lease the land from the Trust Lands Division. If there is no direct descendant, the farm unit would be made available to capable young farmers.

The lease would be renewable every five years at the option of the lessee on a non-competitive basis. The annual lease fee would be 2 percent below the prime rate on the original purchase price paid for the land by the Trust Lands Division. At the end of any five-year lease interval, the lessee would have the right to purchase the land at its current appraised agricultural value.

Under the proposed transfer system, the starting farmer could establish a secure land base. This would allow him to concentrate his investments in equipment, buildings and livestock until the farm unit provides sufficient returns to allow purchase of the land.

While any size farm unit could be purchased by the Trust Lands Division, no lessee could receive a farm unit larger than the average-size farm within an area of comparable land use, productivity and cropping patterns. To avoid a reduction in tax base to local government units, the lessee would be required to pay taxes on land leased from the Trust Lands Division just as if it were his own land.

The lease would require the lessee to be the operator of the leased land and to be a resident of the community in which the land is located. The lessee could not sublease or otherwise rent the land to any other individual. However, the lessee could operate the leased land in partnership with the person who originally sold the land to the Trust Lands Division. This exception would permit a "father-son" type partnership on the leased land.

The Trust Lands Division could lease land to a farm cooperative, provided that all members of the co-op were residents of the community in which the land is located, and that all co-op members would be actually engaged in farming the leased land. The limitation on the amount of land leased to a cooperative would be the multiple of the number of heads of households who are co-op members times the average size farm within that area.

The Community Land Trust

In recent years, great interest has developed in a modern version of an ancient landholding concept, the community land trust. In the following paper, which was presented at the First National Conference on Land Reform, Robert Swann outlines the basic features and advantages of the land trust approach. For more information, the interested reader should write to the International Independence Institute, West Road, Box 183, Ashby, Massachusetts 01431. Swann is director of the Institute.

Robert Swann

The community land trust is a legal entity, a quasi-public body, chartered to hold land in stewardship for all mankind present and future while protecting the legitimate use-rights of its residents.

The community land trust is not primarily concerned with common ownership. Rather, its concern is for ownership for the common good, which may or may not be combined with common ownership. The word "trust" is used more to connote the idea of trusteeship or stewardship than to define the legal form. Most often the land trust will be a non-profit corporation rather than a legal trust.

The following key features differentiate the community land trust from the ordinary real estate trust or conservation trust, and enable it to achieve its goal of "ownership for the common good":

(1) The trust holds land only.

(2) The land *user* is protected by his long-term lease—99 years and renewable.

(3) The *land* itself is protected by the charter of the trust.

215

(4) The trustees do not "control" the users of the land; they implement the trust charter and ensure that the provisions of the charter and of the lease contract are fulfilled.

There are several reasons why land trusts are advantageous in a strategy of regional decentralization. First, trusts can be established immediately. They do not require any legislation for implementation. Land trusteeship utilizes the legal principle of the leasehold, but in perpetuity (99 years and renewable). Such long-term leasehold systems are being utilized increasingly in urban areas (in New York City most skyscrapers are on leased ground) and even in new towns (Irvine, California, for instance), but generally for maximizing profit. In the concept of trusteeship, all profits return to the trust, which in turn can donate them to the community via special agreements.

Second, trusteeship and stewardship can be built on a long tradition in many societies: Indians of North and South America, the *ejidos* of Mexico, the tribes of Africa, the "commons" in England and New England, the Crofters system in Scotland, the Eskimos of Alaska, and in recent history the Gramdan movement in India and the Jewish National Fund in Israel.

A third advantage of the land trust is that it bypasses one of the problems traditionally associated with land reform, *i.e.,* forcible expropriation. Many homeowners are afraid of the term "land reform" because they fear (irrationally) loss of their homes. Such fear is not associated with the words "trust" or "trusteeship," nor is expropriation advocated under the land trust concept. In fact, since trusteeship implies and includes a concern for the land itself in a conservation or ecological sense, new allies can be found in the environmental movement. This creates a basis for a broader political coalition than land redistribution, *per se*.

At the same time, it should be pointed out that under traditional land redistribution, land typically reverts to its former absentee landlords (or new ones) in about twenty years, partly because other factors or forces in the economy (control of money, etc.) are not changed. Under land trusteeship, on the other hand, land is taken out of private ownership voluntarily and placed in trusteeship in perpetuity.

Fourth, a trust can be used as a holding mechanism for all sizes and tracts of land. Some of these tracts may be large enough to build entire new towns, or simply used as farms or conservation tracts. This flexibility permits both short and long range strategies which can include small farms, large farms, or combinations of both. In this way, the modern technology of the large scale farm can be utilized while, at the same time, the trust can encourage and promote new ecological farming systems to avoid the dangers of monoculture and pesticides.

Another aspect of this same issue which must be considered is the assumption that farmworkers and agriculturalists want small farms. I doubt this is true in most cases if it means giving up labor-saving technology. Farm workers want real participation in the ownership of their production, but not at the expense of more stoop labor. In our planning sessions for New Communities, Inc., in southwest Georgia, we ran into this issue any number of times. Farmers did not want to divide the farm (about 6,000 acres) into small individual tracts because it would make the use of machinery more difficult. Cucumbers, which meant a great deal of stoop labor, were voted out as a cash crop even though they bring good prices.

To those who are concerned about chemical fertilizers and pesticides, as well as those who believe in the small farm system, this attitude presents a problem and a challenge. I suggest that a land trust which helps remove the burden of land payments from the back of the farmworker is the best approach to this problem. Since so-called organic farming generally costs more in terms of labor, the farmer is often forced to use pesticides and chemicals on his fields in order to meet his mortgage obligations. In our planning at New Communities we decided to combine large-scale farming with small plots for home gardens and animals. This planning permits families to live reasonably close together in villages where other needs such as schooling, recreation, buying clubs and marketing co-ops can be provided.

In Israel, over two-thirds of the best land is held in trust by the Jewish National Fund. There, everything from small farms, *kibbutzim, moshavim* and whole new towns are planned and established on trust land.

In short, the trusteeship concept is an activist approach to the problem of redistribution of resources, and while it is initially aimed at the land, as it grows and develops as a movement it can begin to reach out into other areas of resource management.

The Importance of Unions

The struggle for justice in rural America will not be won unless poor and landless people organize to build economic and political power. That is the message of Dolores Huerta, vice-president of the United Farm Workers Union, AFL-CIO. She points out that although many small farmers are presently opposed to the farmworker's union, it is in the long run interest of family farmers and farmworkers to join together against big growers and corporations.

Her statement is taken from testimony before the Senate Migratory Labor Subcommittee in 1972. Since she testified, many large growers who had previously signed collective bargaining contracts with the UFW have switched to the Teamsters. To regain those contracts, the UFW has launched new boycotts of non-UFW grapes, lettuce and wines, especially Gallo wines.

Dolores Huerta

The only areas in the United States where the problems of farmworkers have been dealt with are those where we have been able to achieve collective bargaining agreements. In those areas the laws are being enforced. Children are not working, people have protection from discharge, people have drinking water and toilets in the field. They are not being poisoned by pesticides because the law in those areas is enforced by the union stewards and the ranch committee. And, what is more, workers are benefiting from cooperative programs that they themselves have set up.

With all of the millions of dollars in subsidies that growers have received, they have never bothered to establish one social program, a clinic or anything else. We have a clinic staffed by doctors and nurses that is treating eighty farmworkers a day, and it was built by the farmworkers without one penny of federal

218

money or any kind of tax writeoff or subsidy. We have a credit union that lends more than $3 million of farmworkers' money to themselves, the first of its kind in the nation. We have a service program in several states where farmworkers can go with their problems. We have a gasoline station where farmworkers can buy their gas cheaper than they can in town. We have a death benefit insurance program, which is also on a cooperative basis. When you talk about farmworkers' income being only $2,000 or $3,000 a year, a death in the family can be a very devastating thing. We have a program where farmworkers can get a death benefit of $1,000 plus $500 for each dependent.

We are beginning contruction of a village which will be a home for retired Filipino workers who were left abandoned and could not marry because of discriminatory immigration laws and discriminatory state laws. We have a medical plan in our union contract so we get full medical care, including hospitalization and maternity benefits, for working fifty hours under a minimum plan and 250 hours under a major plan. This we have done without any help from the government.

What happens when we don't have collective bargaining agreements? There are no social programs. The growers have complete control of the courts, the law enforcement agencies and other governmental bodies. There is an on-going conspiracy between the government and the growers against the farmworkers. There is no enforcement of the laws about children working or pesticides. Farmworkers can't expect to win in governmental bodies no matter how many laws are made.

We have had farmworkers shot in the face by labor contractors. They have been beaten by growers. They have been beaten by paid hoods. We can't get complaints signed against them. But in the Salines Valley where we had a strike, we had hundreds of workers arrested for picketing. Our director was thrown in jail for twenty-one days because he instituted a boycott. The court issued injunctions to prevent us from doing any kind of picketing, from even having one picket.

Unless we get unions, and farmworkers get strength in rural America, we are not going to get any kind of justice. We will not get enforcement of any law, whether it is the 160-acre limit or the cotton subsidy limit or a child labor law or the disability insurance law.

The same legislators that have hurt farmworkers over the years, beginning with the *bracero* program, are clamoring now to cover us under legislation that would take away the boycott. But it is quite clear to us that the boycott is the only way to win union protection and collective bargaining contracts for farmworkers. We have won many strikes and we have gotten recognition from growers and then they have refused to negotiate and sign a contract. In the lettuce industry we called a moratorium on the boycott and engaged in seven months of negotiations. To this day we don't have a contract and we will probably have to institute the lettuce boycott again. [Ed. note: They did.]

There is something else I want to point out. It has been much easier to unionize the employees of conglomerates and large corporations than those of small growers. Part of this may be because of their vulnerability to boycotts, but another reason is that somewhere in their organization they have somebody who has some kind of a savvy about labor relations. They have somebody in their organization who understands that farmworkers deserve some kind of humane treatment. We don't often have that experience with small growers.

The only corporations that we were able to get contracts with in the lettuce industries are the conglomerates: United Fruit, Inter-Harvest, Purex and D'Arrigo, which is a large, family-owned corporation. In the wine industry we have had the same experience. We are having an awful lot of trouble getting the smaller companies to sign contracts, even though their workers want them. It seems the only way we can force growers who do not negotiate with their workers is to have a product-wide boycott, which takes a tremendous amount of energy and time.

Here, we should note that the trend toward monopolization of the grocery market by a few chains such as Safeway has set in pretty deeply. Agribusiness interests sit on the board of directors of Safeway. Safeway is producing many of the products that they sell, therefore competing directly with the growers that they buy from. The consumer does not have a choice about which products he wants to buy. Safeway makes that decision.

We insist that Safeway has a responsibility to the consumers and to the general public. We insist that Safeway should not sell products that have been gathered from the exploitation of the farmworkers. We insist that Safeway has the responsibility to sell products that have been picked under sanitary conditions. If they have the freedom to grow and monopolize, they also have a corporate responsibility toward farmworkers who produce the food and consumers who buy it. If Safeway does not take the responsibility seriously, then the consumer should boycott their stores.

Another sad situation is that fruits are often left lying in the field. This year there was something like a 60 percent peach drop in California. This was devastating to the growers. It was devastating to the farmworkers who went there to pick that fruit and had no work when they arrived, and also to the consumer who is paying a higher price for his canned peaches. There were oranges which were left unpicked and other fresh produce which was not harvested. Yet poor people in the cities of America cannot afford to buy food.

In many of these cases the grower doesn't have a thing to say about the prices set for the product. This is done completely by the chain stores. When you say to the growers, "Why don't you get together and bargain with the processors," they are afraid the stores might not buy their product. It is sad to think they have the same right to bargain that farmworkers have, but they are unwilling to organize to get their bargaining power going. They want to take their profits out of the sweat of the workers.

The role of growers, shippers, distributors and chain stores is not that of providing an adequate food supply for the nation. It is only geared to profits. So we have a dilemma of agricultural surpluses, hungry people in our land of plenty and give-away programs of billions of dollars to the already-wealthy.

At the lowest rung on the agricultural totem pole, the farmworkers need protection. We need the freedom to continue the unionization without legislative restraints. We need protection from mechanization that will place thousands of farmworkers in the already overflowing ranks of the unemployed. We need exemptions from the wage freeze, just as growers are exempt from the price freeze. And we need to have existing legislation enforced.

I think, finally, we have to have some kind of low-interest financing so that farmworkers and small farmers can form cooperative ventures. It is unfortunate that small growers who are not unionized are so blinded with bigotry against unionization, because we have many problems in common—the lack of bargaining power and political power. Their attitude prohibits our working with them and makes it difficult for smaller growers who do want to work with the union. So we will have to wait until we find ways to organize them. Then we can start talking to each other.

The Family Farm Anti-Trust Act

The effort to ban corporations from farming has its roots in the Populist movement of the late 19th Century. By the 1930s, anti-corporate forces were strong enough in one state—North Dakota—to pass a law prohibiting corporations from farming or owning agricultural land. Within the past few years, three more states—Minnesota, Kansas and South Dakota—have adopted measures restricting the right of corporations to engage in farming. Similar legislation is pending in the legislatures of several other states.

At the federal level, some three dozen senators and congressmen have sponsored the Family Farm Anti-Trust Act, which would ban from agriculture all corporations with more than $3 million in non-farming assets. Here, Oren Lee Staley, president of the National Farmers Organization, explains what the act would do and why it is needed. His statement is excerpted from testimony before the House Judiciary Committee in 1972.

———————————————— Oren Lee Staley

We hear a great deal today about rural development, stopping the out-migration to overcrowded cities, and the amount of money needed through loans, grants or otherwise to make rural communities attractive to our young people. Passage of this bill and reversal of the trend toward corporate farming will do more than any other single legislative action to preserve the rural economy and consequently the welfare of small town businessmen, schools and churches, and the very community life about which so many are concerned.

Perhaps it is important at the outset to consider what this bill does not do. It does not stop any normal farm operation from growing and becoming more efficient. The average business or professional man may still farm as a hobby or, for that matter, may farm seriously without legal interference as long as his total assets are not large enough to make him a threat to competitive farm enterprise.

Farmers are perhaps the strongest champions of free enterprise, competition and independence. They do not fear for one moment the competition of businessmen who operate with the same availability of credit, equipment and talent as we find in family farming. However, concentrated economic power in the hands of integrators sets up unfair competition in terms of working capital, controlled cost/price ratios, use of advantageous tax rate structures and the like.

As compared to individual farm and ranch operators, corporations have distinct advantages that encourage their headlong plunge into farming. They have easy access to funds at lower rates of interest. In many cases, they may buy machinery, fertilizers, fuel and other needed supplies from subsidiaries who are in a position to deliver at lower prices—or at least, they can take advantage of large-scale central purchasing and bypass normal distribution channels. The integrated operation is in a position to produce and sell at cost, or even at lower prices, for two or three years while accumulating and developing land for long-term capital gain. The individual farmer simply cannot compete on these terms.

It is estimated that over half of the corporate farming set-ups in this country have been formed in the last ten years. It is a matter of record that large corporations were able to take over 98 percent of broiler production in fifteen years.

Don F. Kirchner, president and cashier of the Peoples Trust and Savings Bank, Riverside, Iowa and Chairman of the Agriculture-Rural America Committee of the Independent Banker's Association, summed up the challenge facing this country when he said: "If corporation farming is to be controlled, it must be done while there are still relatively few large corporations involved. It must be done before farming, as we know it, is destroyed. It must be done before farming, as we know it, is rural America who wish to enter farming and ranching."

The main thrust of the bill is to prevent corporations, trusts or conglomerates who are in interstate commerce and have assets of more than $3 million from directly or indirectly engaging in farming or ranching. Individuals and partnerships of sufficient size to exercise unwarranted power in violation of the spirit of the antitrust laws are prohibited from agricultural activity.

The prohibition against owning, operating or controlling agricultural production is an effort to separate control of the raw product supply from the processing, handling, shipping and sale of food and fiber products. This would draw the line between production and all that follows in the food chain leading to retail sales.

Charitable, educational and nonprofit institutions engaged in agricultural research are permitted to continue in farming if the producing activity is a part of their normal functions. There is no desire on the part of farmers and ranchers to hinder these worthwhile endeavors. Bona fide cooperatives and associations of farmers are also exempted from the act.

Those who would otherwise not be eligible to farm but who are now in farming would have five years to get out. Any organization or individual coming into ownership of land or other production facilities as a result of loan forfeiture or foreclosure or another legal process may exercise full control but must dispose of the property in two years. These provisions are fair and practical.

Experience indicates that we may not expect vigorous action in the Department of Justice or the Federal Trade Commission to stop the takeover of agricultural production by large integrators. Therefore, this new law authorizes private suits to bring about enforcement.

What a National Land Reform Act Might Look Like

Legislation banning corporations from agriculture is only one side of the land reform coin. In addition to excluding absentee owners from farming, positive steps must be taken to include new low-income people who live and work in rural areas. In short, true land reform involves a transfer of ownership from those who own too much to those who don't own anything.

The following outline of possible transfer mechanisms was prepared by the Center for Rural Studies and presented at the First National Conference on Land Reform.

Center for Rural Studies

A national land reform act would have to accomplish two things: (1) take away control of land and resources from large absentee-owned corporations, and (2) give control to either public agencies, cooperatively or community-owned entities, or low-income individuals. In other words, a land reform act would establish a *transfer mechanism*. In addition, it would provide *supporting institutions and assistance* for new recipients of land and resources.

The best transfer mechanism would be one that (1) minimizes bureaucracy; (2) does not tax the wage-earner or small property-owner; and (3) builds upon existing transfer models.

Three types of transfer mechanism are conceivable. One would be a national *trust fund* which would not itself acquire land but which would make grants to other public and private entities for the purpose of land acquisition. A trust fund can be financed through taxes that fall primarily on the wealthy—in this case, a national severance tax and some form of unearned increment tax would be appropriate. And there are existing models, including a very close one, the Land and Water Conservation Fund.

The Land and Water Conservation Fund gets its money (about $100 million a year) from national park entrance fees, concession rentals, boat licenses, hunting stamps, taxes on guns and ammunition, and some royalties from federal off-shore oil leases. This money is used to buy land for parks, recreation and wildlife refuges. A national severance tax and unearned increment tax could enormously expand such a land transfer fund, in terms of both revenue and purpose.

A national severance tax of 5 percent could raise about $700 million annually, according to Senator Lee Metcalf, who has proposed such a tax. The potential of an unearned increment tax is even greater. According to the National Commission on Urban Problems, chaired by former Senator Paul Douglas, land values in the 1960s went up $25 billion a year. By now the annual increment is probably close to $50 billion. A 10 percent tax would yield $5 billion.

The revenues from these taxes could be granted to federal and regional agencies, states, cities, co-operatives, CDCs, Indian tribes and non-profit land trusts for the purchase of land and energy resources from large absentee owners. Funds would be distributed geographically according to a formula that considers such factors as population, income levees and degree of concentrated land ownership. Funds would be allocated categorically in accordance with another formula such as the following: 50 percent for parks, open space recreation and wildlife refuges; not more than 15 percent each for productive farmland, timber, energy resources and land for housing and new communities.

Another possible transfer mechanism is a *land bank*. Under a land bank system, the recipients of land and resources would pay for them over a lengthy period, perhaps forty years, with payments waived for the first five years. Interest rates would be low—perhaps 2 percent, as with REA loans, or even 0 percent, as with loans to irrigation districts for construction of canals. Or repayment might be a percent of future earnings, the way some colleges provide for repayment of tuition loans. Front money would come from congressional appropriations.

The major difference between the *land bank* and the *trust fund* is that the latter puts the financial burden on existing wealthy owners of land and resources, while the former puts it on future recipients, who are likely to be poor. Also, a land bank would depend on annual appropriations, while a trust fund, once established, would finance itself relatively automatically. It would, of course, be possible to combine the two approaches, using earmarked taxes *and* congressional appropriations to finance land purchases, and giving both 100 percent grants *and* low-interest loans.

A third possible transfer mechanism would be a *national trust*. The trust would purchase land using regular appropriations and/or special taxes such as the severance and unearned increment tax. It would not re-sell land but rather lease it on a long-term basis to family farmers, co-operatives, CDCs, etc. A model would be the Jewish National Fund in Israel (although this is a private land trust). The questions raised by the trust approach are: (1) Are Americans ready to give up the tradition of private land ownership in favor of long-term leases? And: (2) What kind of bureaucracy would be required to administer the land held by a national trust, and how would such a bureaucracy relate to the Interior and Agriculture Departments?

Redistributing land would not, by itself, make land reform work. Additional assistance would have to be provided to make sure that the present trend toward elimination of small landholdings did not repeat.

Among the forms of assistance needed are: (1) seed capital; (2) cheap credit; (3) technical assistance; (4) marketing assistance. These might be provided by existing agencies, or possibly by a new agency such as a revived Farm Security Administration. In addition, protection against reconcentration might be provided in the form of acreage limitations, tax and/or anti-trust provisions.

Buying Back the Land

As the previous article suggests, and as John McClaughry points out elsewhere in this book, an excellent way to effect land reform is through a tax-supported land acquisition trust fund. Here, Peter Barnes describes in detail how such a trust fund might operate. The selection is adopted from a lengthier article that appeared in the Summer 1973 issue of Working Papers.

Peter Barnes

It is just within the realm of possibility that low-income groups, by joining with environmentalists, labor and other progressive forces, can bring about a better distribution of land. The mechanism for doing this could be a series of state government trust funds which, for purposes of public salability, might be called Land Conservation Funds (LCF).

An LCF would make land acquisition funds available for uses consistent with environmental protection and economic justice. It would do so without imposing new levies on most taxpayers. It would thus be a much stronger political device than is presently available for land acquisition and control. With relatively minor modifications, the LCF model could also be adopted at the federal level.

An LCF would not itself own land, operate farms, or set up local enterprises. These functions would be filled by other public and private institutions, some of which already exist, many of which still need to be built. An LCF would be a *politically salable transfer mechanism* that would make *financially possible* a redistribution of land. Its uniqueness is that it would do so in a way not dependent upon the diminishing willingness of the legislatures (or Congress) to tax the working and middle classes for the benefit of the poor.

Here's how an LCF would work. Like the highway, social security, and other existing trust funds, an LCF would be a separate government account into which money would pour from special taxes—in this case, taxes that fall not on the average taxpayer but on the wealthy few who profit most from land and resources. Revenues from these taxes would be allocated for carefully specified purposes and recipients: half would go to cities, towns, counties and regional park districts for the purchase of open space land; the remainder would be granted to low-income cooperatives, community development corporations (CDCs), public utility districts and non-profit land trusts for the purchase of productive land. Like other trust funds, an LCF, once established, would be self-perpetuating and relatively immune to political sabotage.

The principal taxes feeding an LCF would be a severance tax on the extraction of oil, gas, other minerals and timber, and a tax on the unearned increment in land value. The severance tax is a well-known tax applied in many mineral-rich states, including Texas, Louisiana, Oklahoma and Alaska. The unearned increment tax is a kind of capital gains tax applied to land. It has been used in England, South Africa, Australia, Denmark and other countries, and was recently adopted in Vermont. Its name derives from what John Stuart Mill called the "unearned increment"—the rise in land value brought about by public expenditures (highways, sewers, irrigation projects, etc.) and by economic and population growth. Capturing the unearned increment for private gain is what land speculation is all about. Recapturing it for the public good is the objective of an unearned increment tax.

A state severance tax would fall most heavily on the holders of working interests in oil, natural gas, cement, sand and gravel, other mineral properties and timber—*i.e.*, the major oil, timber and landowning companies. Since these companies benefit from a wide variety of federal and state tax preferences—and since the resources they extract are a gift of nature to all, not to just a privileged few—a severance tax is a highly appropriate levy. From an environmental standpoint, the severance tax is an excellent one because, unlike the *ad valorem* property tax, it encourages conservation rather than depletion of resources. For added effect a differentially high rate might be applied to the severance of resources (such as virgin redwoods) deemed particularly worthy of conservation.

The unearned increment tax, if universally applied, would be borne by all owners of land that is appreciating in value. It would be wise, however, to exempt land immediately related to most residential property, small farms and small businesses. The tax would then be borne almost entirely by large landowning corporations and real estate speculators. Its impact would be greatest on large owners of urban and urban fringe land.

In practice, an unearned increment tax could take a variety of forms. The National Commission on Urban Problems, chaired by former Senator Paul Douglas, described several, ranging from a total shift to site value taxation to a transaction tax on land value increments. I favor tacking on an annual land gains tax to the state income tax. This would be similar to the ordinary capital gains tax except that it would be payable while gains accrue, rather than at time of realization—a necessary difference since one objective of the tax is to induce large absentee landowners to sell.

Collection of an annual land gains tax would be relatively simple. Local assessors, when mailing out their annual property tax bills, would make two extra carbon copies; one would be mailed to the property owner, the other to the state revenue agency for verification purposes. Each non-exempt property owner would then submit a self-declaratory land gains schedule along with his state income tax return. He would attach to this schedule copies of all appropriate property tax bills, much as employers' W-2 forms are attached to the regular income tax form. His tax liability would be calculated in the following fashion: from the current total value of his non-exempt real estate he would subtract the total value as of the preceding year. Then he would subtract the amount expended on capital improvements during the preceding year, and add the depreciation (if any) claimed elsewhere in his return. This would yield the land value increment for the previous year—i.e., the increase in value not attributable to the owner's own improvements—which would then be taxed at an appropriate rate.

Exemptions might be structured as follows: the first $40,000 worth of a taxpayer's owner-occupied home, plus the first $40,000 worth of an owner-operated farm or business property, plus an equivalent value for each rental unit owned, would be excluded in computing the land gain. In addition, the first $1,000 in gain would be exempt. People who owned no property (or only owner-occupied homes worth less than $40,000) would not have to file a land gains schedule. Over 95 percent of households would thus be spared direct contact with the tax, while the rental exemption would avoid a shifting of its burden onto tenants.

The revenue potential of a land gains tax would be considerable. Consider the following data for California. Land in California is rising in value at about 8 percent per year. That creates an initial tax base of about $7.5 billion. Approximately half of that would be excluded under the residential, small farm and small business exemptions. That leaves about $3.7 billion that could be subject to uniform, progressive or differential tax rates. A flat 10 percent rate would yield $370 million annually; a 15 percent rate would yield $555 million.

Besides raising money to buy back the land, an annual land gains tax would, by itself, have several desirable consequences. By diminishing the tax advantages of investing in land, it would encourage the wealthy to put their money elsewhere, and perhaps prompt present large owners of land to begin selling. This would create a downward impact on land prices—downward enough (if the tax rate were reasonable) to slow the natural rate of increase but not to depress land values below their current level. To some extent this downward pressure would diminish the revenues raised by the tax, but it would also make buying land cheaper for LCF recipients.

Another consequence of a land gains tax would be the creation of jobs and housing. This would occur because a tax on land gains does not discourage productive investment. In fact, it encourages construction of income-producing improvements on land, especially in the central city and on the urban fringe. Because of the exemption for low and middle-income homes and rental units, the greatest incentive would be to build low and middle-income housing, as opposed to luxury highrises, shopping centers and office buildings. If a differentially high rate were applied to land rezoned for higher use, the incentive would be to construct new housing in areas already zoned for it, rather than to sprawl into still-unspoiled areas. If the housing were built by low-income co-ops or CDCs that received land acquisition funds through an LCF, housing costs could be cut as much as 30 percent.

Three objections to the land gains tax might be: (1) it does not allow for appreciation attributable to inflation; (2) it taxes unrealized gains; and (3) it constitutes double taxation, since land gains would be taxed while accruing, then again by the state and federal governments when realized. These objections are readily answered. (1) No correction for inflation is allowed in taxing inflation-induced increases in wages, dividends, interest or ordinary capital gains, so why should landowners be entitled to special treatment? (2) Any large landowner who did not have sufficient cash to pay the tax on unrealized gains could easily sell a portion of his holdings without hardship. In any case, the ordinary *ad valorem* property tax, which constitutes a heavier burden than would a land gains tax, is worse than an unrealized gains tax because it taxes property values annually even when gains are not accrued. (3) The double tax argument is unconvincing because the "double tax" is not more than a higher rate of taxation on capital gains, a rate that *in toto* would still not equal the rate of taxation on wages. Moreover, taxes paid to a state LCF would be deductible from federal income taxes.

Who would get the money to buy land, and how would allocations be made?

The law establishing an LCF would contain a formula for allocating funds by purpose, type of recipient, and location. Thus, 50 percent of the revenues might be allocated for open space acquisition. These funds would be divided among state agencies, cities, towns, counties and regional park districts in accordance with population density, quality and quantity of open space available, and other factors. Some funds would be used for preserving wilderness and wildlife refuges, some for recreational areas, some for urban parks and suburban greenbelts (in which land might be leased back to small farmers and co-ops). Grants from the LCF could cover up to 100 percent of land acquisition costs.

The remaining 50 percent of LCF revenues would be divided among the following types of recipients:

—Cooperatives of low-income families, for the acquisition of land for agriculture, related enterprises and housing. For example, farmworkers might wish to buy out a corporate farm and run it cooperatively.

—Community development corporations in rural and urban areas, for the acquisition of land for housing and non-polluting industries.

—Public utility districts, for the acquisition of land, water or energy resources.

—Non-profit land trusts, similar to the Jewish National Fund in Israel, for the acquisition of land for lease to family farmers and rural cooperatives, or of common land for Indian tribes and Mexican-American *ejidos.*

As with open space funds, grants to private recipients could cover up to 100 percent of land costs. Recipients would thus be free of debt burden on their land, and could use their land as collateral to borrow money for farm equipment, housing supplies and other capital outlays. The debt-free gift of land would be in the tradition of the Homestead Act. It would, of course, be a subsidy, but one that would barely match the subsidies and tax breaks given to railroads, cattle barons, timber companies, energy corporations, wealthy tax-loss farmers, real estate developers and the like.

Grants by an LCF to private recipients would be subject to a number of restrictions and conditions. First, carefully drafted language in the law would assure that recipient corporations, cooperatives and land trusts would either be genuinely nonprofit or owned in major part by persons of low or moderate income who lived and worked in or near the enterprises involved.

Second, nonprofit trusts receiving grants would be permitted to lease only to resident farmers and cooperatives. In no event could a trust lease farmland to an absentee operator, nor could it lease more than 320 acres of irrigated farmland, or 1,000 acres of unirrigated farmland, to the same family, or double that amount to the same cooperative. In leasing farmland the trust would give preference to people with farm work experience and low incomes. Violation of any of these conditions would cause for revocation of all grants, with grant money repayable (with interest plus a penalty) to the LCF. Co-ops and CDCs would be subject to similar restrictions.

Third, all recipients would be barred from resale of LCF-funded land for at least fifteen years. After that time the LCF would retain first option to purchase at a price not greater than its initial grant, plus an allowance for inflation.

What would happen if something like an LCF were established today? Would co-ops, CDCs and nonprofit land trusts be able to handle a million acres if they received them, free of debt burden, next week or next year? Sadly, I suspect that the answer is no. There is an immediate, desperate need to improve the management capabilities of community and cooperatively owned enterprises, and to increase the readiness of low-income families to participate meaningfully in such undertakings. Government, university, foundation and other private resources should be poured into this task.

Politically, however, I think we are much further along than many people realize. Voters in California, their sensitivities heightened by smog, sprawl and environmental activism, approved a statewide coastal zoning initiative in 1972 as well as numerous local open space bond issues. (School bond issues, meanwhile, were generally going down to defeat.)

The Republican county executive of Suffolk County, New York, recently proposed that the county buy up farmland threatened with subdivision and lease it back to the farmers who are using it. A report financed by Laurance Rockefeller recommended creation of "public corporations" to acquire land for new town development. Robert Wood, former secretary of Housing and Urban Development and now president of the University of Massachusetts, has said that "public ownership and public planning are probably the essential components for a genuine land reform program."

Many if not most of these "land reformers" see public land ownership as beneficial primarily to profit-seeking new town developers, bankers and well-to-do farmers, rather than low-income groups. In my view, public land ownership is not a very promising device for helping poor people, although it's fine for open space preservation. Helping the poor requires that they have more direct access to the land than public ownership *per se* has provided or can provide. The point, however, is that people are ready, or almost ready, to accept the notion of buying back sizable quantities of land from its present owners. The political task is to make sure that "buy-back-the-land" programs are not used solely for parks and commercial developers, but are also designed to benefit low-income and community groups.

What is necessary over the next few years, it seems to me, is a two-front strategy. On the political front, we must deal with the fact that voters are prepared to spend public money to purchase land for migratory birds, but not yet to do the same for migratory workers. While lamenting and fighting this reality we might as well take advantage of it; there are no other sources of large-scale money for community economic development on the horizon.

The second front involves developing the psychological and managerial capabilities necessary for running new economic structures such as cooperatives, CDCs and land trusts. This is a much more difficult task than the political one, and a persistent problem over the next few years will be that of timing—how to develop social structures fast enough to keep up with the political gains I believe are possible.

It would be wrong to conclude on too optimistic a note. The forces opposed to genuine land reform are powerful. If locally owned economic institutions are to survive, much less to flourish, there must be more than a redistribution of land. There must also be far-reaching changes in federal tax, subsidy and anti-trust policies. Such changes will be extremely difficult to bring about. It can only be said at this time that the possibilities are there. It is up to us to work strenuously for their attainment.

A Farmworker Speaks

It seems fitting to close this book not with a complicated proposal for legislation, but with the simple words of a farmworker. No one has more eloquently stated the case for land reform than Manuel Leon, one of the founders of a small grape growing co-op in Ripon, California. Leon testified in Spanish at the Senate Migratory Labor Subcommittee hearings in Fresno. Here are his words, translated into English.

Manuel Leon

Many words have been written and many promises have been made to my people. According to the promises, I was to be fully educated, employed in a job that was paying a better than average salary, have all of the benefits and protections enjoyed by the accepted citizen, and be in a position to borrow whatever money I might need to start a business of my own.

We are not jealous of the millions of dollars that are granted to rich farmers to hold back production, nor the millions given to railroads and aircraft companies to cover up thefts and bad management. Even the billions spent on trips to the moon, Mars and the space shuttle do not upset us because that is beyond our comprehension. We think only in terms of the thousands of dollars that we hope will be invested in human lives and not in cold machines.

There is so very little that we ask for. The great majority of our people do not want things given to us free. We prefer to work for what we get. As it is, a day does not pass that a charity worker or a neighbor does not press us to apply for free assistance, food stamps or free medical care from the authorities. We do not desire this. We desire to make it on our own either through employment or through self-employment.

It is a matter of record that many of us have all but managed the ranches at which we have been employed. In most cases we have been given the job of preparing the soil for planting; have been left to determine the amount of nutrients needed to bring

235

the soil to a productive level; and, finally, have had to apply the nutrients. The jobs of planting, irrigating, pruning, thinning, spraying, fertilizing and nurturing the soil have not been done by the average big farmer. Outside of an occasional visit by the owner, the entire operation in most ranches is left to the trained *campesino*. Late at night, while we are struggling to keep a secondhand tractor, a dull disc harrow or a dilapidated plow in workable condition in some windswept barn under a dim light, we feel despair and frustration because we are so aware that the farmer inside the house enjoying the warmth of his living room could have been us.

To put it in simple words, we, the *campesinos,* have been for years the backbone of agriculture. How many times have I seen only a sea of brown faces pruning, thinning or picking, and how many times have I heard the farmer sigh a sigh of relief when we showed up? The irony is that as a reward we are being cursed as revolutionaries, are being sprayed with sulfur because we demand better wages and working conditions, and, finally are being denied the basic rights of health insurance, unemployment insurance, and the right of all rights, the opportunity to put together a business of our own.

Gentlemen, I want to be very frank with you. This is a very difficult thing for me to say because I am not accustomed to making demands. My trust has always been in God and I have always left all things to Him. But now, deep in my heart, I feel that He is pressing me to ask for this one thing. Please, gentlemen, make it possible for my people to buy their own land and to care for it with hands that are full of love for the soil. As a simple man I do not know how this can be done. But if it is, we will be able to build a life for ourselves that will make this country more fruitful and more aware that, unlike others, we have never resorted to violence to bring about change.

Thank you for allowing me to reveal the depths of my heart.

Burt Fox. *Lettuce harvest; California, 1972.*

The American farmworker

© George Ballis. *Farmworker; California, 1968.*

Dorothea Lange, FSA. *Filipinos cutting lettuce; California, 1935.*

*...can be lifted from poverty and protected
from exploitation*

© George Ballis. *Farmworkers; Puerto Rico, 1969.*

Bob Fitch. *Salinas short hoe; California.*

... by farmworker unions and small-scale co-operatives.

Larry Rana, USDA. *Migrant farmworker and housing; New York, 1967.*

USDA. *Child playing with toaster, 1967.*

Bob Fitch. *First box of union grapes; California, 1970.*

Bob Fitch. *United Farm Workers pickets talk with grape workers; California.*

John Vachon, FSA. *Young farmer; Minnesota, 1940.*

Rex Gogerty. *Young farmer; Iowa, 1974.*

Russell Lee, FSA. *Owners of Co-Op thresher; Utah, 1940.*

The small farmer can be similarly helped.

T. L. Gettings. *Maine, 1973.*

T. L. Gettings. *California, 1974.*

Bob Griffith. *Pennsylvania, 1974.*

T. L. Gettings. *Colorado, 1974.*

T. L. Gettings. *Michigan, 1974.*

Rodale Press. *Iowa, 1974.*

T. L. Gettings. *North Carolina, 1974.*

*There can be a place for the little person
in the United States.*

T. L. Gettings. *Michigan, 1974.*

T. L. Gettings. *California, 1973.*

Bob Fitch. *Agribusiness in California.*

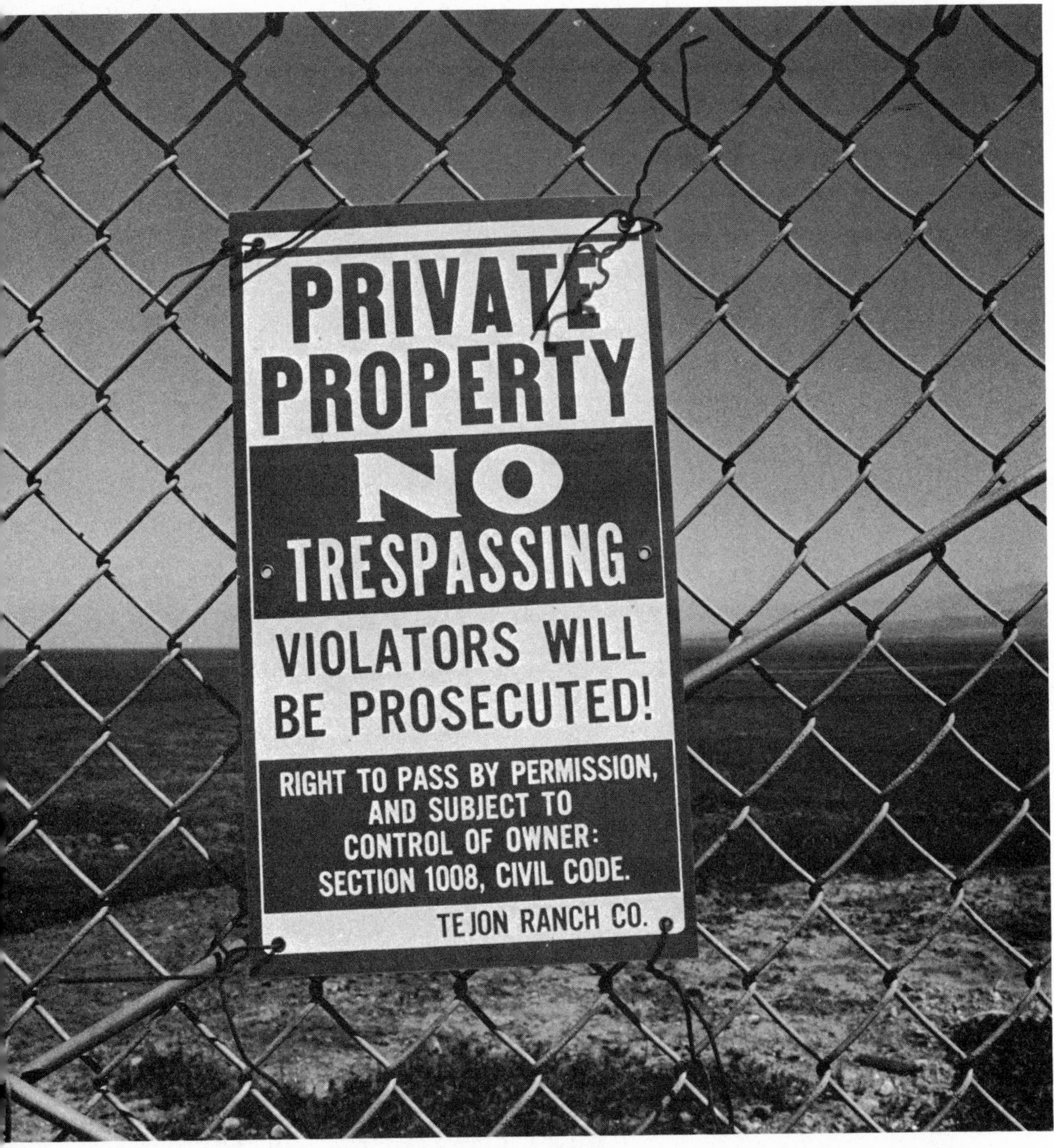

Bob Griffith. *Pennsylvania, 1974.*

A Note About
the National Coalition
for Land Reform

The National Coalition for Land Reform is an organization of family farmers, farmworkers, environmentalists and other citizens from all sections of the country who recognize the need for a more equitable distribution of land. Coalition members believe that ownership of land by those who work and live on it is a key to alleviating poverty, easing urban overcrowding, reducing welfare costs and unemployment, protecting the environment and building a stronger democracy.

The Coalition has its national office along Rural Route 4, Creston, Iowa 40801. Readers are invited to become members of the Coalition and to receive *People & Land*. Membership is $10 a year.

All royalties from the sale of this reader will be used to support the political and educational activities of the Coalition.

Index

Abourezk, Sen. James, 127
Abrahamsen, Martin A., 207
Absentee ownership, 33, 48-55, 139-43, 189, 255. See also Agribusiness; Railroads, land ownership and control; Coal, land holdings and mining.
Adams Ranch, 178-80
Agribusiness, 39, 44-45, 48-50, 81-95, 121, 174-75, 177, 190, 204, 208, 220, 223-25
Agribusiness Accountability Project, 81, 89, 139
Agricultural College Act, 8
Agricultural Stabilization and Conservation Service, 179
Agriculture-Rural America Committee, 223
Alabama, 36, 118, 189
Alaska, 152, 229
Alcalde, Calif., 15
Allis-Chalmer Corporation, 92
American Farm Bureau Federation, 20
American Historical Review, 7
American Indian Press Association, 56
American Legion, 115
American Metal Climax Corporation, 46-47
American Veterans Committee, 115
AMTRAK, see Railroads
Apache Corporation, 141
Appalachia, land use in, 33-39; mineral wealth, 152-53. See also Poverty, rural.
Appalachia Lookout, 144
Appalachian Mountain Authority proposal, 36
Arizona, 56, 88, 114, 145
Arkansas, 118
Army Engineers, 115
Aroostook County (Me.), 55
Arvin, Calif., 171-75
Associated Farmers, 173
Associated Press, 180-81
Atlantic Richfield Corporation, 141
Atomic Energy Commission, 123
Augusta, Ga., 146

Baker Driveaway Company, 178
Bank for Cooperatives, 41
Bankhead-Jones Farm Tenant Act, 18
Betterment levy, 157-58
Big Black Mountain, 145
Big Sky Corporation, 45
Black Economic Research Center, 40
Blacks, 184, 190, 211, land ownership in South, 40-42 migration to North, 41
Bloomfield Hills, Mich., 178
Blue Ridge Mountains, 37
Boulder Canyon Reclamation Project, 114

Bowman, Larry, 38
Boycotts, 209, 219-20
Bridge, William Oldfield, 179-81
Brown, Edmund G., 116
Brown, John Nicholas, 49
Brown Land Company, 49
Bureau of Agricultural Economics (U.S.), 171, 173. See also Department of Agriculture (U.S.).
Bureau of the Budget (U.S.), 189
Bureau of Indian Affairs (U.S.), 58, 60
Bureau of Reclamation (U.S.), 46, 58, 115, 123, 127
Burlington Northern Railroad, 45-46
Burt County (Neb.), 49
Buttes Gas and Oil Corporation, 141

California, 9, 82, 86-87, 114, 115, 122-24, 126, 142, 148-51, 171-75, 220, 230, 233, 235, 256. See also specific place names.
California Assembly Select Committee on Open Space Lands, 148
California Land Conservation Act, see Williamson Act
California Water Project, 123
Cal-Maine Foods Corporation, 141
Campbell Soup Corporation, 81-82
Campesinos, 235-36. See also Farmworkers; Migrant workers.
Capital gains tax, 229
Carroll County (Va.), 37-38
Carroll News, 38
Cascade Mountain, 38
Case, J. I., Corporation, 92
Cedar Rapids, Ia., 48
Center for Community Economic Development, 40
Center for Rural Affairs, 48
Center for Rural Studies, 149, 225, 256
Central Valley project, 114-15
Champion-U.S. Plywood Corporation, 146
Chase Manhattan Corporation, 52
Chavez, Cesar, 204. See also Migrant workers; United Farm Workers.
Chelan County (Wash.), 35
Chemicals in food, see Food additives
Chevron Corporation, 46-47
Cheyenne Indians, 44, 47
Chicanos, 211, 232. See also Migrants.
Coal, land holdings and mining, 33-37, 45
Coal, land holdings and mining, 33-37, 45-47, 56, 123-24, 125-27, 144-45, 152-53. See also United Mine Workers.

Collective land ownership, 42-43
Colorado, 9, 115, 120-21, 123, 126
Colorado-Big Thompson Project, 114
Colorado River, 58-59, 116
Community Development Corporation (CDC), 226, 229, 233, 234
Community land trust, 215-17. See also Collective land ownership.
Concord, Vt., 154
Confucius, 143
Congress (U.S.), see names of specific Senators, Representatives, Departments, and Committees.
Connecticut, 81
Conservatism, definition, 19
Consol Corporation, 45-46
Constitution, U.S., 171
Consumers Cooperative Association, see Farmaldn Industries
Continental Oil Corporation, 128
Cooperativa Campesina, 203-206, 207
Cooperative development, 153. See also Farm cooperatives.
Cooperative Refinery Association, 209
Cooperatives, see Farm cooperatives
Corporate farming, see Agribusiness
Cowden, Howard A., 209
Crow Indians, 44, 47

Danielson, Sen. George, 149
D'Arrigo Corporation, 220
Dakotas, 44
Davis, Kenneth S., 209
Del Monte Corporation, 82-83
Department of Agriculture (U.S.), 49, 82, 84-86, 88, 90, 99, 171, 180, 190, 205-206, 227
Department of Defense (U.S.), 42, 204
Department of Health, Education and Welfare (U.S.), 187
Department of Housing and Urban Development (U.S.), 233
Department of Interior (U.S.), 12, 14-15, 42, 47, 58-60, 114, 123, 126, 227
Department of Justice (U.S.), 58-59, 224
Department of Labor (U.S.), 187
Department of Treasury (U.S.), 189
Depletion taxes, 153
Desert Land Act, 8
Des Moines Sunday Register, 177, 180
Developers and land development, 37-39, 44-45, 52-53, 148-50. See also names of specific companies.
Dinuba, Calif., 171-75
Douglas, Sen. Paul, 115, 226, 230
Dow Chemical Company, 210

257

Eagle River Case, 59
Economic Development Administration, 182
Economic Opportunity Act, 189
Ector County (Tex.), 146
Eisenbacher, Father Linus, 179
Elkhorn Coal Corporation, 145
Energy crisis, 122-27
Energy sources, 36, 97-98, 122-24, 125-28. See also Coal; Minerals
England, see Great Britain
Engle formula, 115
Environmental preservation, 148-51, 157. See also Land reform.
Eskimos, 216. See also Alaska.
Evans, George Henry, 5

Fair Labor Standards Act, 183
Family Farm Anti-Trust Act, 222-24
Family farms, see Landowners, small or individual
Farm cooperatives, 203-206, 208, 211-12, 218, 224, 226, 232-33. See also names of individual cooperatives.
Farmer Cooperative Service (U.S.D.A.), 205-206, 207
Farmer's Home Administration, 189
Farmers Home Administration Act, 19
Farmers Union, 115
Farmland Industries, 209-212. See also Farm cooperatives.
Farm Machinery, 91-93, 98, 206
Farms, Appalachia, 37-39
Farm Security Administration, 17-19, 227
Farmworkers, 92, 203-206, 219-21, 235-36. See also Landowners, small or individual; Migrant workers
Federal Land Bank, 50
Federal Oil and Gas Corporation, proposal, 127
Federal Power Commission, 126
Federal Trade Commission, 82, 224
Filipino workers, 219. See also Chicanos.
First Midwest Land Conference, 48
First National Conference on Land Reform, 17, 33, 52, 113, 152, 154, 215, 225. See also Land reform.
Fleischmann's Corporation, 85
Flint Hills, Kans., 50
Flood control, 113, 118-19. See also Reclamation projects; Water rights.
Food additives (chemical), 83-85, 86-88, 96-99
Food advertising, 81-85, 86-88, 93-94
Food production system, 81-85, 86-88, 96-99
Forest lands, 10-11, 45, 52-53. See also Timber companies.
Forfeiture acts, in U.S. Congress, 13, 14
Fort Mojave Tribal Council, 58-59
Fortune, 149, 209
Fresno County (Calif.), 87
Future Farmers of America, 210-11

Gallo wines, 218
Gas, natural, 34, 125-26. See also Energy sources.
Gates, Paul Wallace, 48
General Accounting Office (U.S.), 189
General Foods Corporation, 82
General Mills Corporation, 82
General Services Administration, 61
George III, 52
George, Henry, 154-55
Georgia, 146, 189, 217
Georgia Pacific Corporation, 190

Geothermal energy, 124, 125-27; sites, 126
Getty Oil Corporation, 126
Gladstone, William Ewart, 116
Gold Kist, Inc., 208-209
Goldsmith, Oliver, 7
Good Humor Ice Cream, 85
Grande Ronde Indians, 60
Grange, The, 115
Grant County (Wash.), 35
Grazing lands, 8, 12, 44-45, 120-21
Great Britain, 7, 157-58; taxes, 157-58, 229
Great Lakes region, 9-10, 184
Green Giant Corporation, 82
Griswold, Erwin N., 59
Greeley, Horace, 51
Groundhog Mountain Developers Corporation, 37-38
Gulf and Western Corporation, 52
Gulf Oil Corporation, 46-47, 128
Gwaltney Smithfield, see IT&T

Hanford, Calif., 149
Harlan County (Ky.), 145, 190
Harris, Sen. Fred, 171
Harriss, C. Lowell, 157-58,
Hart, Sen. Philip, 127
Hartford Life Insurance Corporation, 142
Hatch Act, 89
Health insurance, 236
Hepburn Railroad Act, 46
Heublein Inc. Corporation, 81
Highlander Research Center, 33
Homestead Act, 7-11, 16, 40, 42, 44, 172, 232
House Judiciary Committee, 222

Ickes, Harold L., 114, 116
Imperial Valley, 87, 114
Increment value tax, 154-57, 226, 229-31. See also Capital gains tax.
Independent Banker's Association, 223
Indian Trust Council Authority, proposal, 59
Indians, land ownership and land rights, 9, 10, 45, 51, 56-61, 216, 226, 232; water rights, 58-60. See also names of specific tribes.
Insect control, 84, 90, 98
Institute for Development of Indian Law, 56
Institute for Liberty and Community, 154
Inter-Harvest Corporation, 220
Interior Department, see Depart
Interior Department, see Department of Interior (U.S.)
Internal Revenue Code, federal, 156
Internal Revenue Service, 142, 180, 181
Intake Water Company, see Tenneco Corporation
International Agricultural Fair, 207
International Harvester Corporation, 92
International Independence Institute, 215
International Paper Corporation, 52, 190
IT&T Corporation, 52, 81
Iowa, 87, 176-81
Irrigation, see Water rights
Irvine, Calif., 216
Israel, 216, 217, 227

Jefferson County (Miss.), 190
Jenkins, Minerva, 58
Jewish National Fund, 216, 217, 227, 232
John Deere Corporation, 92
Johns Manville Corporation, 190
Johnson, Lyndon B., 182

Justice Department, see Department of Justice (U.S.)

Kaiser Aetna Corporation, 141-42
Kansas, 9, 50-51, 222
Kansas City, 210-11
Kansas Farm Project, 48
Kaplan, Doug, 149
Kaplan, Jacob M., 211-12
Kellogg Corporation, 82
Kennedy, Sen. Edward, 59, 127
Kentucky, 36, 152, 188, 190
Kern County (Calif.), 87
Kerr McGee Corporation, 46
Kings County (Calif.), 149
Kings River, 115
Kirby Corporation, 146
Kirchner, Don F., 223
Klamath Indians, 60
Knott County (Ky.), 144-45

Labor-Management Relations Act, 183
LaFollette, Sen. Robert M., 115
Lake Tahoe, Calif., 15
Lakin, Charles, 179-80
Land and Water Conservation Fund, 226
Land bank, 191, 226-27
Land Conservation Funds, 228-32
Land grant colleges, 83, 89-95, 96-99
Landowners, small or individual, 3-4, 17-18, 37-44, 48, 50, 85-88, 92, 96-99, 171-75, 205-208, 210, 222-24. See also Farm cooperatives.
Land reform, 39, 157, 191, 216, 225-27, 228-34, 235-36, 256
Latin America, land reform in, 191
Lawrence, Kans., 48
LeDioyt Land Company, 49
Lee, John, 82
Lehman, Amer, 120
Loesch, Harrison, 59
Louisiana, 118, 152, 229
Louisville Courier-Journal, 145
Lumber companies, see Timber companies
Lumbering, in Appalachia, 34-35

McGovern, Sen. George, 127
McIntyre, Sen. Thomas, 127
McKnight, Father A. J., 206
Madden, J. Patrick, 86
Madison, James, 3
Maine, 52-55, 146, 190
Marion County (Kans.), 51
Maryland, 36
Massey-Ferguson Corporation, 92
Mayer, Dr. Jean, 84
Merrill Lynch, Pierce, Fenner and Smith Corporation, 52
Metcalf, Sen. Lee, 127, 153, 226
Mexican-Americans, see Chicanos
Mexico, 216
Middle West, flood control, 118
Michigan, see Bloomfield Hills
Migrant workers, 203-206, 234-36
Migration, 41, 51, 182, 188
Mill, John Stuart, 229
Minerals, rights and mining, 8, 12, 14, 33-37, 45-47, 125
Minimum wage law, 190
Minnesota, 88, 189, 222
Mississippi (state), 118
Mississippi Delta, 118, 188-90
Mississippi valley, 9-10
Mobility strategy, 187, 188
Mobil Oil Corporation, 46, 128
Mondale, Sen. Walter, 127
Montana, 44-46, 56
Montana Beef Industries, 141
Morales, Tereso, 203-205
Morrill Acts, 89
Morton, Rogers C. B., 12
Moss, Sen. Frank, 127
Mountain Eagle, 33

Nader Task Force on California Land, 150
National Academy of Sciences, 123
National Catholic Rural Life Conference, 115
National Coal Association, 153
National Coalition for Land Reform, 12, 256. See also Center for Rural Studies.
National Commission on Urban Problems, 226, 230
National Farmers Organization, 222
National Farmers' Union, 20, 86, 120
National Irrigation Congress, 114
National Steel Company, 145
Nation's Restaurant News, 82
Navarro, Alfred, 206
Nebraska, 9, 48-49
Needles, Calif., 15
Negroes, see Blacks
Nevada-Truckee Project, 114
New Communities, Inc., 217
New Deal, 17-20, 114-15
New England, 88, 184
New Hampshire, 52-53
New Leader, the 207
New Market, Tenn., 33
New Mexico, 9, 189
Newton, Tex., 146
New York Mining Company, 145
Nixon, Richard M., 59
North Dakota Farmers Union, 213-14
North Central Power Study, 46
Northern Cheyenne Landowners Association, 47
Northern Pacific Railroad, 44-45
Northern Rockies Action Group, 44

Occidental Petroleum Corporation, 126
Odebolt, Ia., 176-81
Office of Economic Opportunity (U.S.), 52, 187, 189, 204-205
Ogallala Reservoir, 120-21
Oil Companies, 44, 45, 53, 120, 125-28, 142, 144, 209-10, 229. See also names of specific corporations.
Oil shale mining, 123-24
Oklahoma, 152, 229
Oppenheimer Industries, 142
Oregon, 9, 82, 87
Organic Gardening and Farming, 84, 96
Owl Creek, Wyo., 115

Pacific Coast states, 10
Pacific Gas and Electric Corporation, 127
Pacific Power and Light Corporation, 46
Paiute Indians, 60
Pan American Union, 121
Peabody Corporation, 46-47
Pennsylvania, 36
Pepperidge Farm Bakery Corporation, 81
Permian Basin, 146
Pesticide, see Insect control
Phillips Petroleum Corporation, 126, 128
Pierce, S.S., Company, 203-204
Pigeon Falls co-Op Creamery, 208
Pike County (Ky.), 144-45
Pillsbury Corporation, 82
Populist movement, 222
Poverty
  rural, 33, 40-42, 50-51, 53, 90, 92, 171, 182-89, 191
  urban, 182, 185
Pre-emption Acts, 5, 8
President's Commission on Rural Poverty, The, 182-86
Preston, Homer, 205
Property tax, see Taxes, property and land

Property transfer tax, 158
Public utility districts, 35-36, 127; 232
Purex Corporation, 220

Quaker Oats Corporation, 82

Railroads, land ownership and control, 8-16, 44-45, 51, 114, 232. See also names of specific railroads.
Reclamation Act, 172
Reclamation Lands Authority, proposal, 117
Reclamation projects, 113-17
Resettlement Administration, 17
Revenue Acts, 139-41
Rheinfrank, June, 180
Richmond County Property Owner's Association, 146
Rio Grande, 58
Rockefeller, Laurance, 233
Rodale, Robert, 84
Roosevelt, Franklin D., 17-20, 115. See also New Deal.
Rosenthal, Harry, 180
Rowe, Jonathan, 150

Sac County (Ia.), 180-81
Safeway Corporation, 220
St. Louis Post Dispatch, 144
St. Regis Paper Corporation, 190
Salinsas Valley, 219
Salt River Project, 114
Salmons, Carl, 38
San Francisco, Calif., 15, 127
San Joaquin Valley, 15, 122, 173
San Jose, Calif., 15
San Luis Valley Project, 115
Santa Clara valley, 148
Santa Maria, Calif., 115
Santa Monica Mountains, 148
Saskatchewan Land Bank Commission, 213
Scotland, 216
Scott Paper Corporation, 52
Seeger, Mike, 38
Senate Migratory Labor Subcommittee, 7, 96, 118, 182, 187, 218, 235
Senate Select Committee on Equal Educational Opportunity, 144
Senate Small Business Committee, 120
Senate Subcommittee on Migratory Labor, see Senate Migratory Labor Subcommittee
Severance tax, 152-53, 226, 229. See also Increment value tax; Tax reform.
Sewall, Joseph, 146
Shaw, Gaylord; 180
Shell Oil Corporation, 45-47, 126\$
Shell Oil Corporation, 45-47, 126
Shinrone Farms, Inc., 177, 180
Siletz Indians, 60
Sioux Indians, 56
Smith-Lever Act, 89
Snyder Harry, 180
Social Security Act, 183
Solar energy, 97, 124-25
South, land use in, 17-18, 20, 40-43, 118-19. See also Flood control; Poverty, rural; Blacks.
South Carolina, 189
South Dakota, 222
Southern Pacific railroad, 14-16, 141
Southwest, poverty in, 184
Spanish Peaks, 45
Spencer, Richard, 146
Speculation, land, 5, 6, 8-11, 33, 51, 52, 54, 119, 155, 156
Standard Brands Corporation, 85
Standard Oil of California Corporation, 126, 128

Standard Oil of Indiana Corporation, 128
Stearns, Wesley, 46
Stock Raising Homestead Act, 44
Strip mining, see Coal mining
Suffolk County (N.Y.), 233
Sunkist Corporation, 211
Sun Oil Corporation, 126
Supreme Court (U.S.), railroad land decisions, 13-16

Taxation, methods of and uses, 45-46, 54, 60, 89, 93, 139-43, 144-47, 148-51, 152-53, 157-58, 225-26, 229-34. See also names of specific taxes.
Taxes
Abuses, 144-47, 158
  exemptions, deductions, and losses, 54, 60, 94, 139-43, 229-33
  payers, 92, 147
  policies and laws, 139-43, 155, 189, 191
  property and land, 3, 46, 119, 139-43, 144-47, 148-51, 154-59, 181, 229-34
  reform, 139-43, 147, 150-51, 152-53, 154-59, 191, 229-34
Tax Institute of America, 155-56
Tax Reform Act, 142
Tax Reform Research Group, 150
Teamsters Union, 218
Technology and food, 82-85, 90-99
Tenneco Corporation, 82-83, 123, 204
Tennessee, 36, 145
Tennessee Valley Authority (TVA), 36, 127
Texaco Corporation, 128, 146
Texas, 87, 115, 146, 152, 188, 229
Thompson River, 46
Timber and Stone Act, 8
Timber companies, 8, 10-11, 34-35, 52, 144, 146, 229, 232. See also Forest lands; names of specific companies.
Timber Culture Act, 8
Timber lands, see Forest lands
Tourism industry, 37-39, 53. See also Developers and land development.
Transfer mechanism, 225, 228. See also Land reform.
Transportation Act of 1940, 14
Tres Pinos, Calif., 15
Truman, Harry S., 115
Trust fund, national, 225-28. See also Land reform.
Tugwell, Rexford Guy, 17

Udall, Stewart L., 116
Unearned increment tax, see Increment value tax
Unemployment, 184. See also Poverty.
Unemployment insurance, 185, 236
unilever Corporation, 85
Union Oil Corporation, 126-28
Union Oil Cooperative, 209
Unionization, 174-75, 221. See also names of specific unions.
United Farm Workers Organizing Committee, 204
United Farm Workers Union, 218-21
United Fruit Corporation, 220
United Mine Workers Union, 153
U.S. Coal and Coke, see U.S. Steel Corporation
U.S.D.A., see Department of Agriculture (U.S.)
U.S. Steel Corporation, 46, 145, 190
Urban
  centers, 171
  land, 229
  poor, 182, 185

Urbanization, 174
Ute Indians, 60

Vermont, 52-53, 156-58, 229
Veterans of Foreign Wars, 115
Virginia, 3, 36
Vogt, William, 121

Walker, Mabel, 154-55
Walthill, Nebr., 48
War on Poverty, 187
Washington (state), 9, 35, 82, 188
Washington Post, 203

Water rights, 113-24
Watsonville, Calif., 203
Welch, Charles, 211
Welch Grape Juice Cooperative, 211-12
Welch, Ronald, 149
Wellford, Harrison, 84
Wells Fargo Bank, 205
Westmoreland Corporation, 46-47
West Virginia, 36, 152, 189
Whitesburg, Ky., 33
Wilderness Act, 45

Wildlife Service (U.S.), 58
Williamson Act, 148-51
Wind-power generation, 97, 124
Wisconsin, 208
Wood, Robert, 233
Working Man's Advocate, The 5
Working Papers, 228
Workman's compensation laws, 183, 185
Wyoming, 44, 127

Yellowstone River, 123

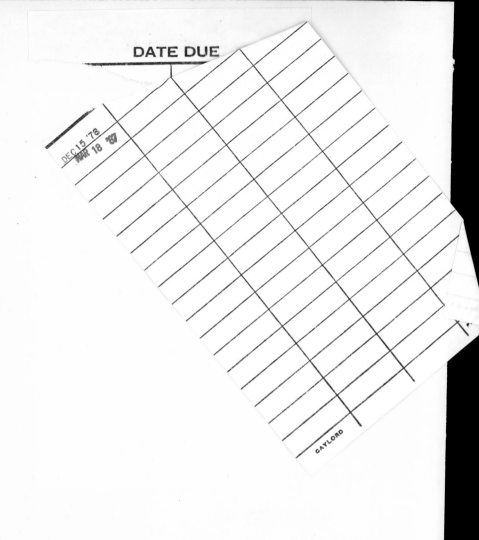